MEDICAL BREAKTHROUGHS
X-RAYS
A GRAPHIC HISTORY

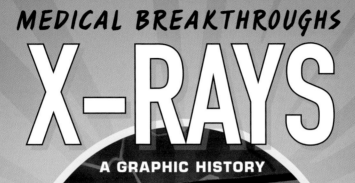

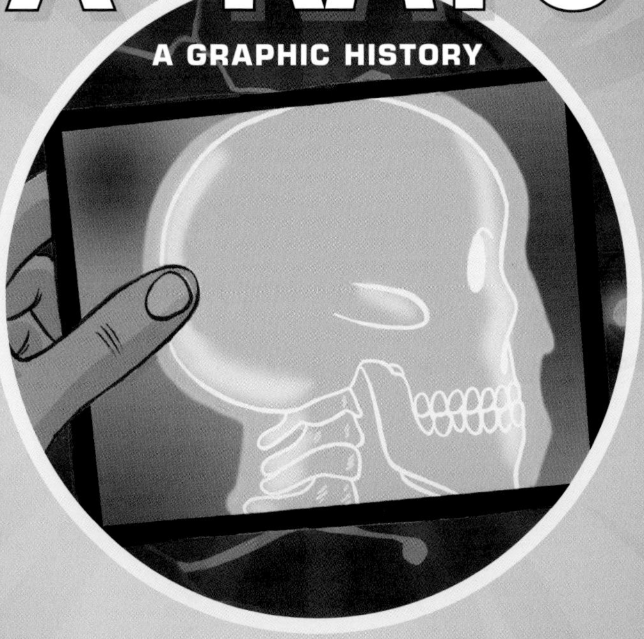

RACHAEL L. THOMAS

ILLUSTRATED BY JOSEP RURAL

GRAPHIC UNIVERSE™ • MINNEAPOLIS

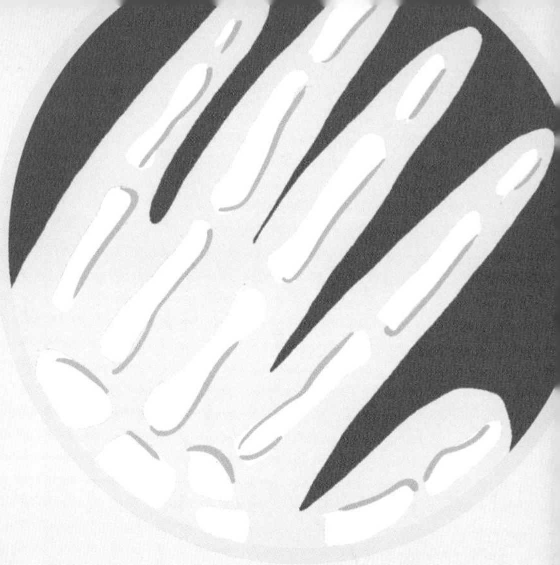

Graphic Universe™
An imprint of Lerner Publishing Group, Inc.
241 First Avenue North
Minneapolis, MN 55401 USA

For reading levels and more information, look up this title at www.lernerbooks.com.

Main body text is set in Dave Gibbons Lower. Typeface provided by Comicraft.

Library of Congress Cataloging-in-Publication Data

Names: Thomas, Rachael L., author. | Rural, Josep, illustrator.
Title: X-rays : a graphic history / Rachael L. Thomas ; illustrations by Josep Rural.
Description: Minneapolis : Graphic Universe , [2022] | Series: Medical breakthroughs | Includes bibliographical references and index. | Audience: Ages 8–12 | Audience: Grades 4–6 | Summary: "With X-rays, doctors detect problems human eyes can't see and even treat illnesses. This graphic history covers the discovery of X-rays, the spread of safety standards, and the start of digital X-rays and 3-D imaging"— Provided by publisher.
Identifiers: LCCN 2021013774 | ISBN 9781541581548 (library binding) | ISBN 9781728448732 (paperback) | ISBN 9781728444154 (ebook)
Subjects: LCSH: X-rays—Juvenile literature. | Radiography—Juvenile literature.
Classification: LCC RC78 .T46 2022 | DDC 616.07/572—dc23

LC record available at https://lccn.loc.gov/2021013774
LC ebook record available at https://lccn.loc.gov/2020455394

Manufactured in the United States of America
1 – CG – 12/15/21

TABLE OF CONTENTS

CHAPTER 1

INSIDE THE HUMAN BODY

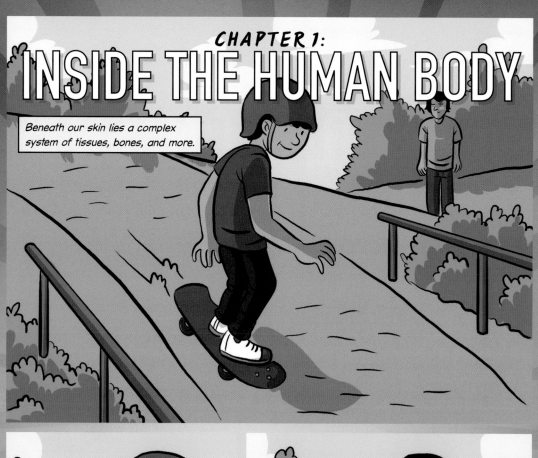

Beneath our skin lies a complex system of tissues, bones, and more.

Is it broken?

Maybe. We'll need to get an X-ray.

We cannot see everything that goes on inside the body. But with X-rays, doctors can spot problems that the human eye cannot detect.

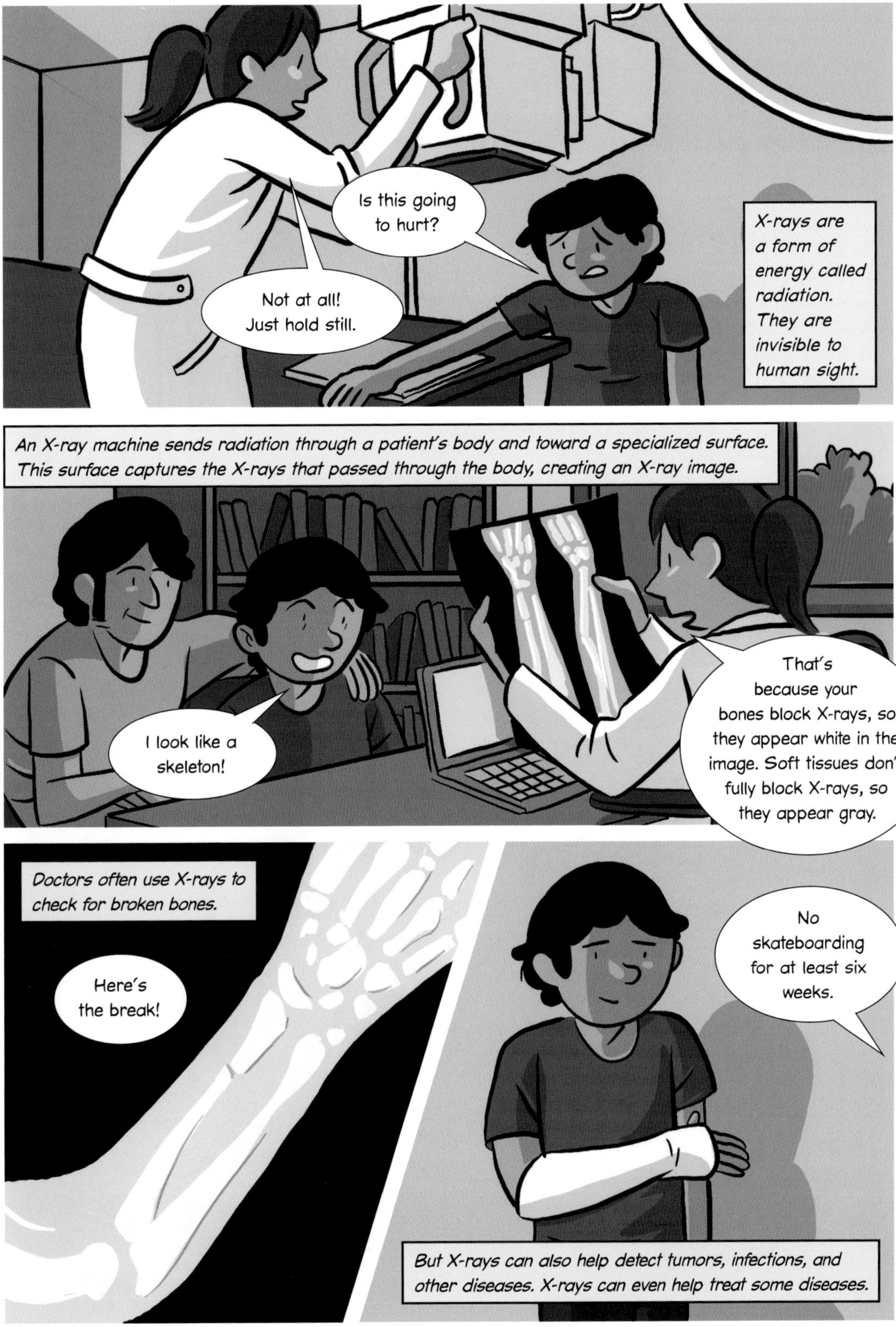

Is this going to hurt?
Not at all! Just hold still.
X-rays are a form of energy called radiation. They are invisible to human sight.
An X-ray machine sends radiation through a patient's body and toward a specialized surface. This surface captures the X-rays that passed through the body, creating an X-ray image.
I look like a skeleton!
That's because your bones block X-rays, so they appear white in the image. Soft tissues don't fully block X-rays, so they appear gray.
Doctors often use X-rays to check for broken bones.
Here's the break!
No skateboarding for at least six weeks.
But X-rays can also help detect tumors, infections, and other diseases. X-rays can even help treat some diseases.

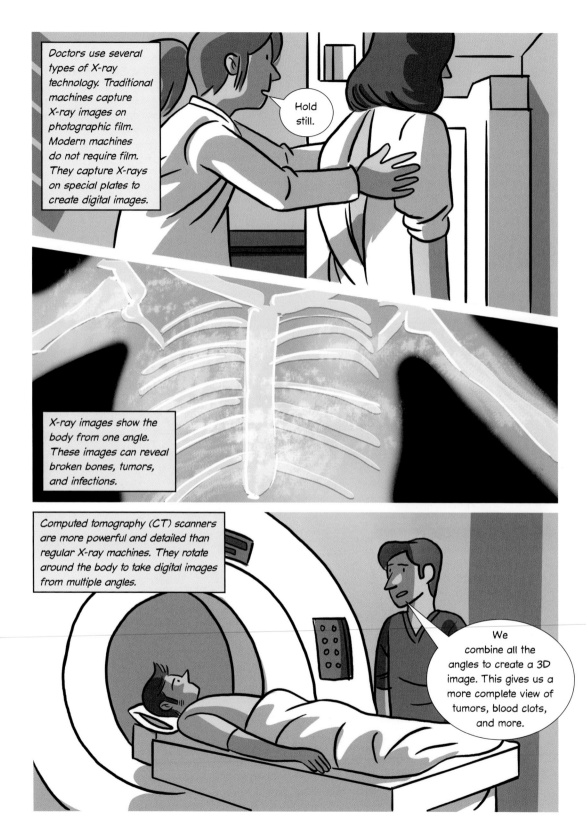

Doctors use several types of X-ray technology. Traditional machines capture X-ray images on photographic film. Modern machines do not require film. They capture X-rays on special plates to create digital images.

Hold still.

X-ray images show the body from one angle. These images can reveal broken bones, tumors, and infections.

Computed tomography (CT) scanners are more powerful and detailed than regular X-ray machines. They rotate around the body to take digital images from multiple angles.

We combine all the angles to create a 3D image. This gives us a more complete view of tumors, blood clots, and more.

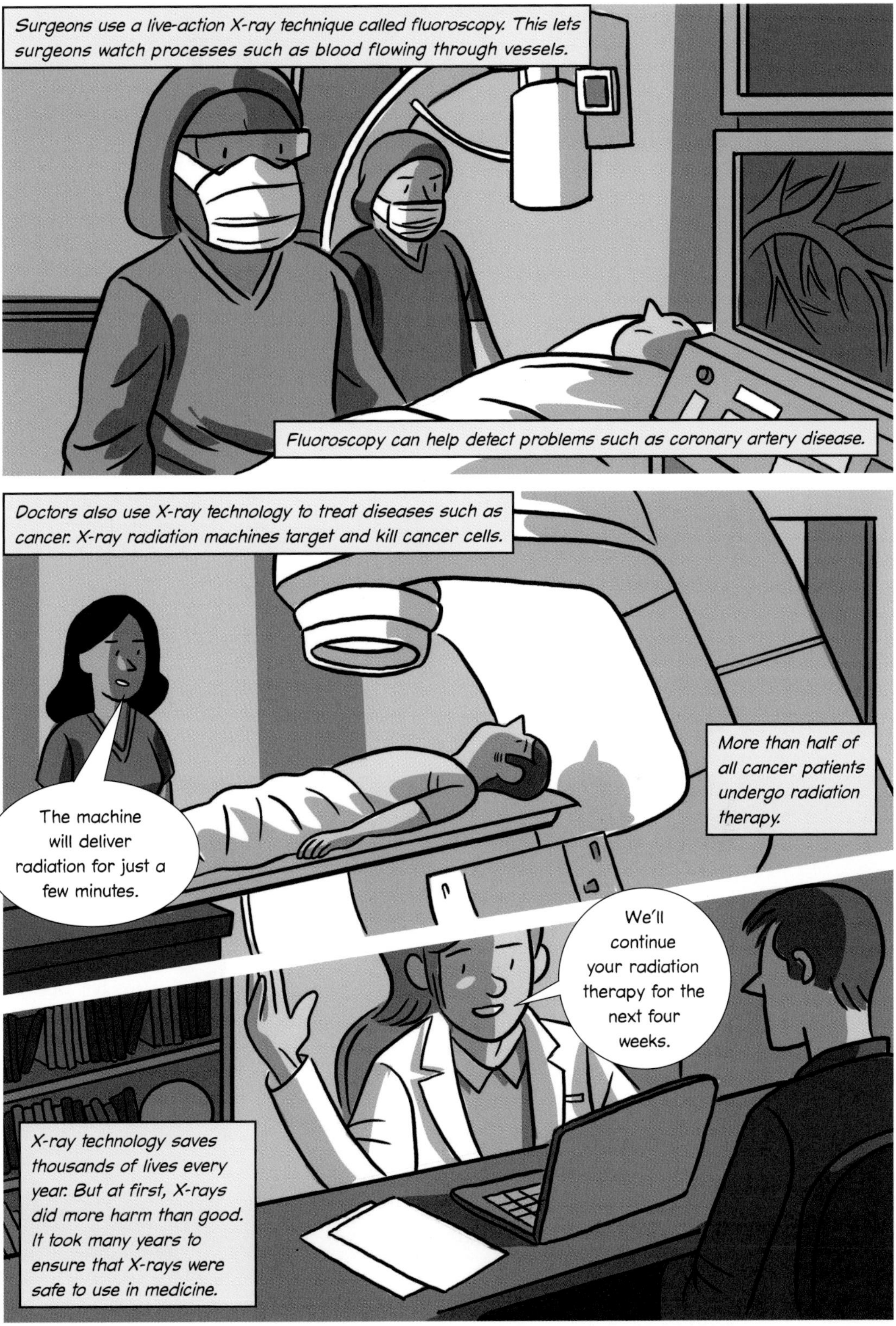
Surgeons use a live-action X-ray technique called fluoroscopy. This lets surgeons watch processes such as blood flowing through vessels.
Fluoroscopy can help detect problems such as coronary artery disease.
Doctors also use X-ray technology to treat diseases such as cancer. X-ray radiation machines target and kill cancer cells.
The machine will deliver radiation for just a few minutes.
More than half of all cancer patients undergo radiation therapy.
We'll continue your radiation therapy for the next four weeks.
X-ray technology saves thousands of lives every year. But at first, X-rays did more harm than good. It took many years to ensure that X-rays were safe to use in medicine.

CHAPTER 2: CROOKES TUBES AND X-RAYS

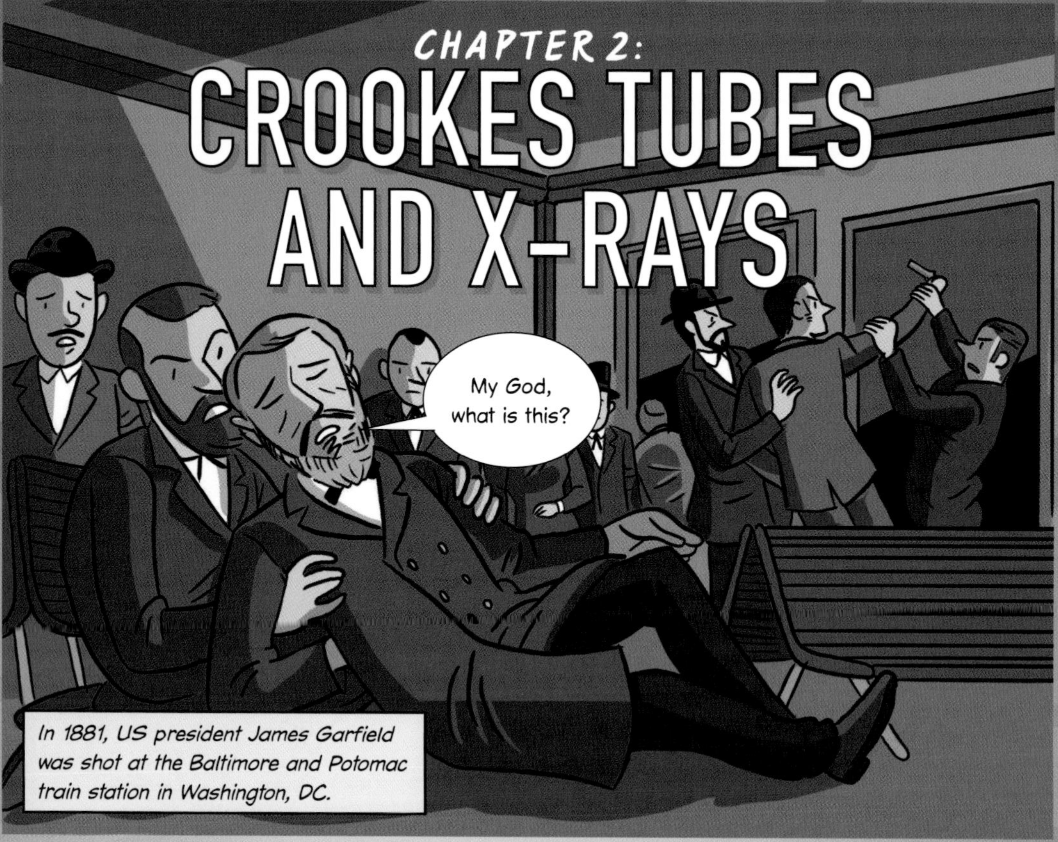
My God, what is this?
In 1881, US president James Garfield was shot at the Baltimore and Potomac train station in Washington, DC.

Garfield's doctors tried to locate the bullet by sticking their fingers into his gunshot wound. At the time, doctors rarely wore gloves. Surgeries were often dangerous and unclean.

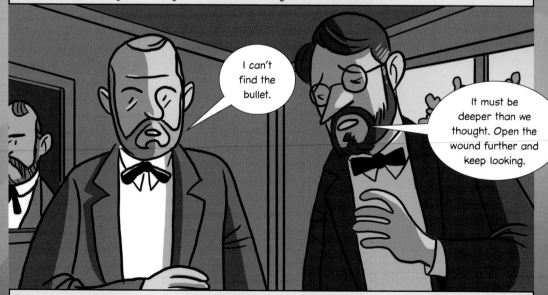

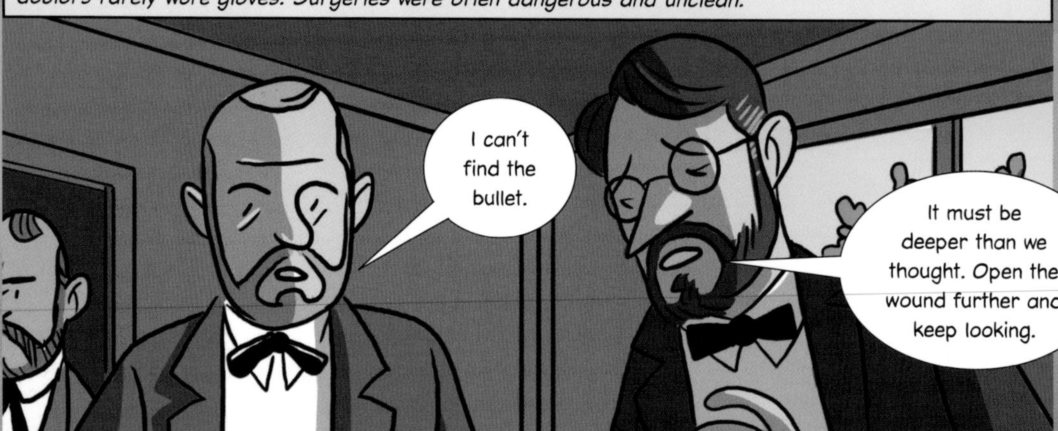
I can't find the bullet.
It must be deeper than we thought. Open the wound further and keep looking.

For weeks, doctors failed to locate and remove the bullet lodged inside Garfield. The wound became infected. More than two months after the shooting, Garfield died.

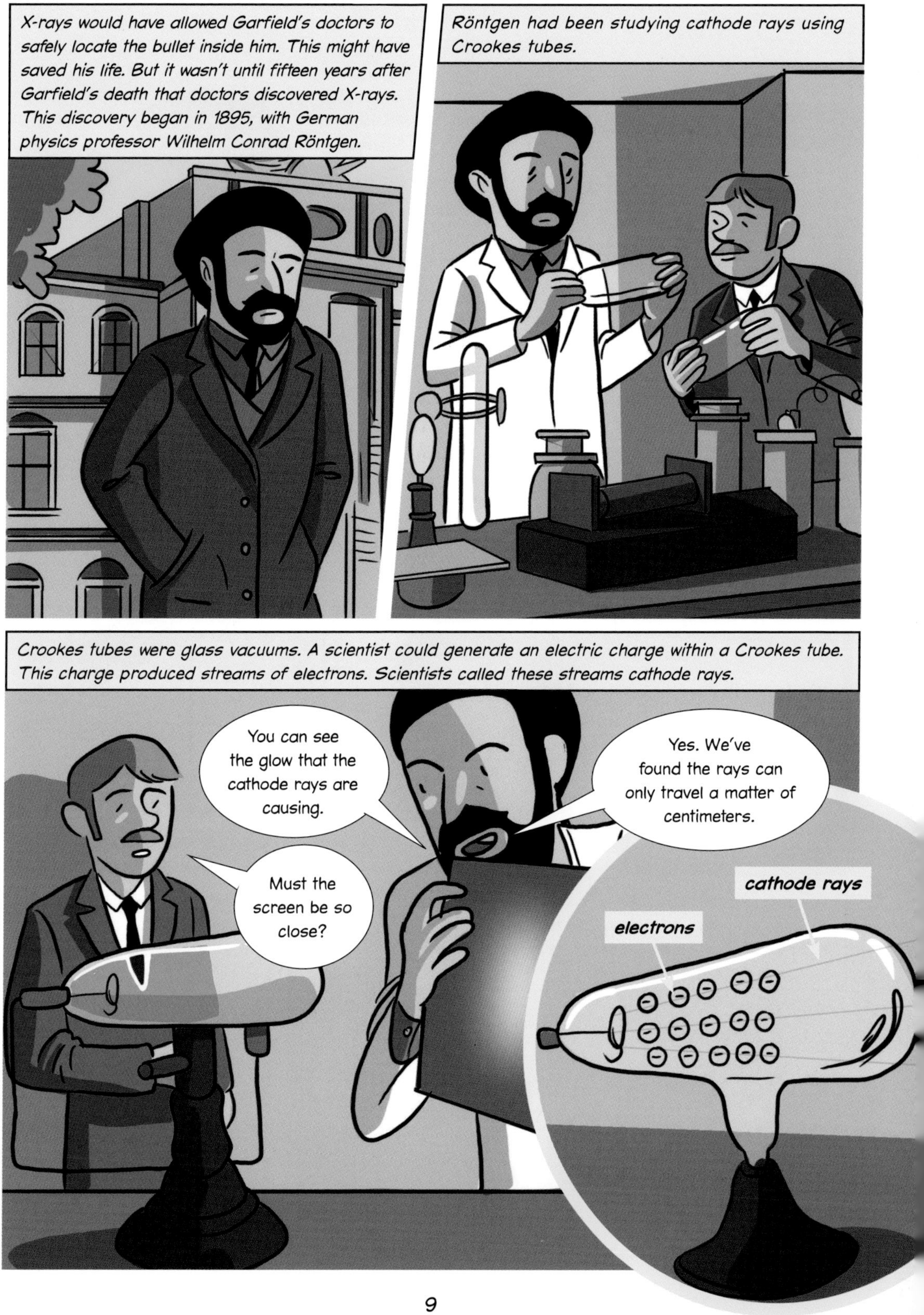
X-rays would have allowed Garfield's doctors to safely locate the bullet inside him. This might have saved his life. But it wasn't until fifteen years after Garfield's death that doctors discovered X-rays. This discovery began in 1895, with German physics professor Wilhelm Conrad Röntgen.
Röntgen had been studying cathode rays using Crookes tubes.
Crookes tubes were glass vacuums. A scientist could generate an electric charge within a Crookes tube. This charge produced streams of electrons. Scientists called these streams cathode rays.
You can see the glow that the cathode rays are causing.
Must the screen be so close?
Yes. We've found the rays can only travel a matter of centimeters.
cathode rays
electrons

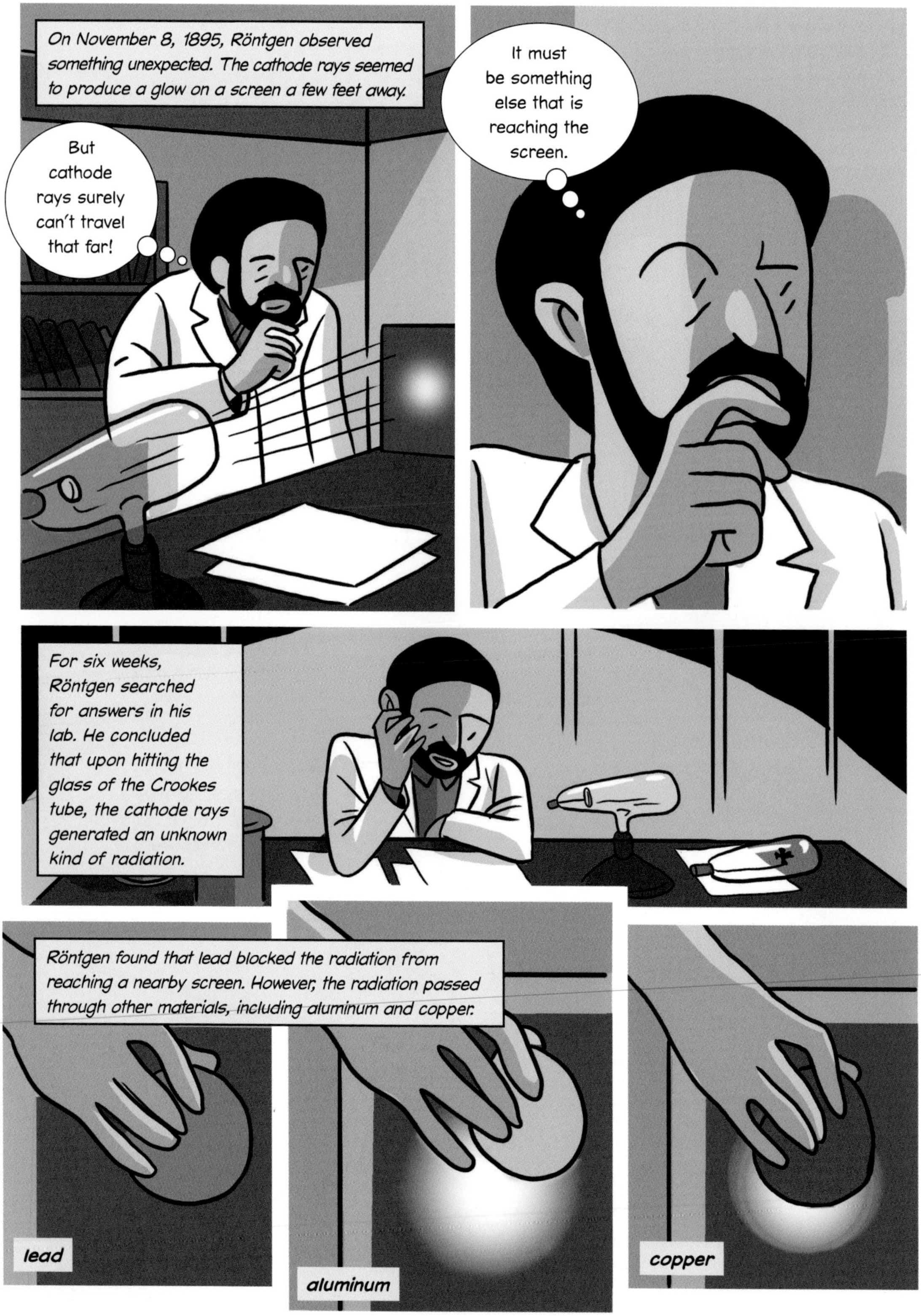
On November 8, 1895, Röntgen observed something unexpected. The cathode rays seemed to produce a glow on a screen a few feet away.
But cathode rays surely can't travel that far!
It must be something else that is reaching the screen.
For six weeks, Röntgen searched for answers in his lab. He concluded that upon hitting the glass of the Crookes tube, the cathode rays generated an unknown kind of radiation.
Röntgen found that lead blocked the radiation from reaching a nearby screen. However, the radiation passed through other materials, including aluminum and copper.
lead
aluminum
copper

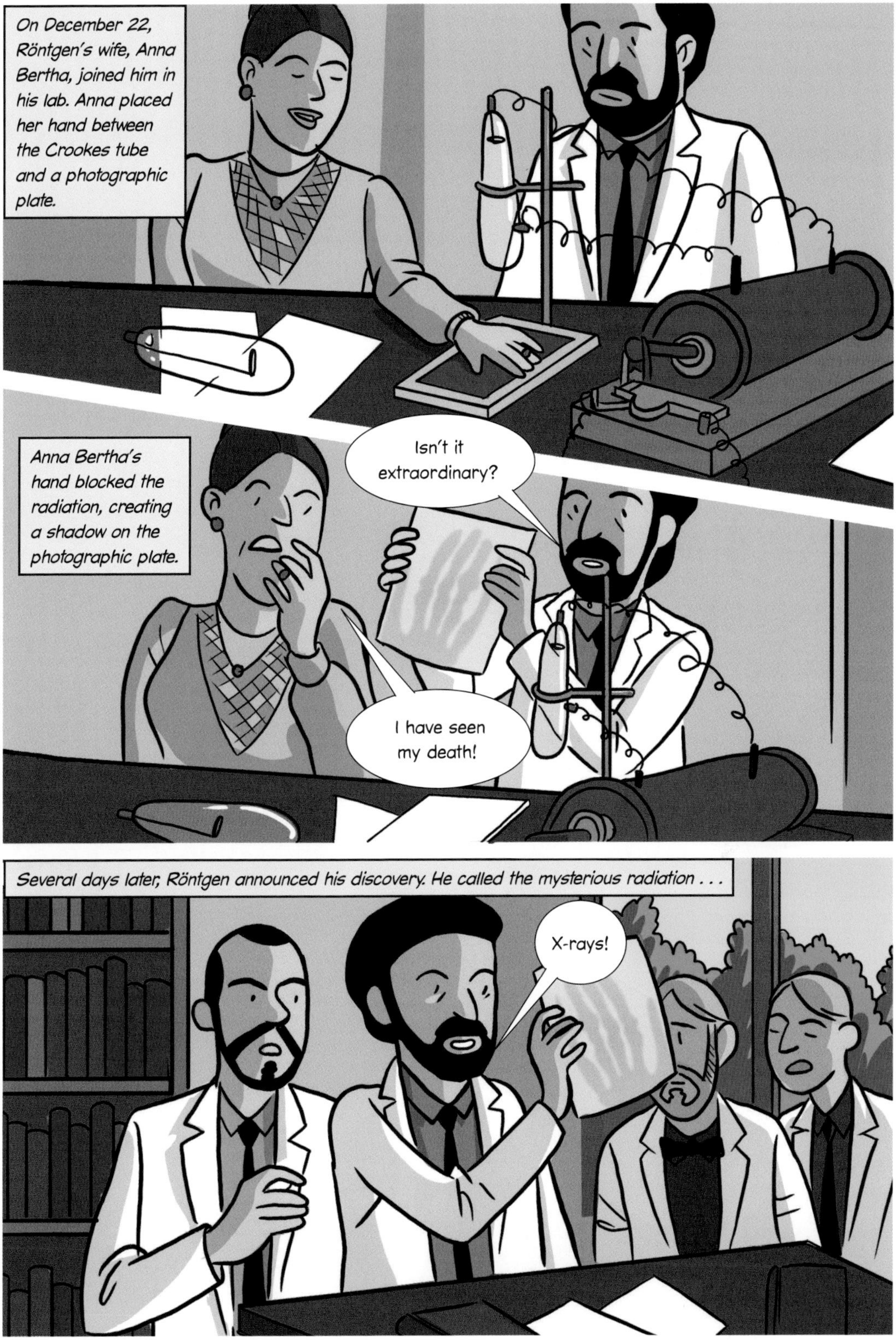

On December 22, Röntgen's wife, Anna Bertha, joined him in his lab. Anna placed her hand between the Crookes tube and a photographic plate.
Anna Bertha's hand blocked the radiation, creating a shadow on the photographic plate.
Isn't it extraordinary?
I have seen my death!
Several days later, Röntgen announced his discovery. He called the mysterious radiation . . .
X-rays!

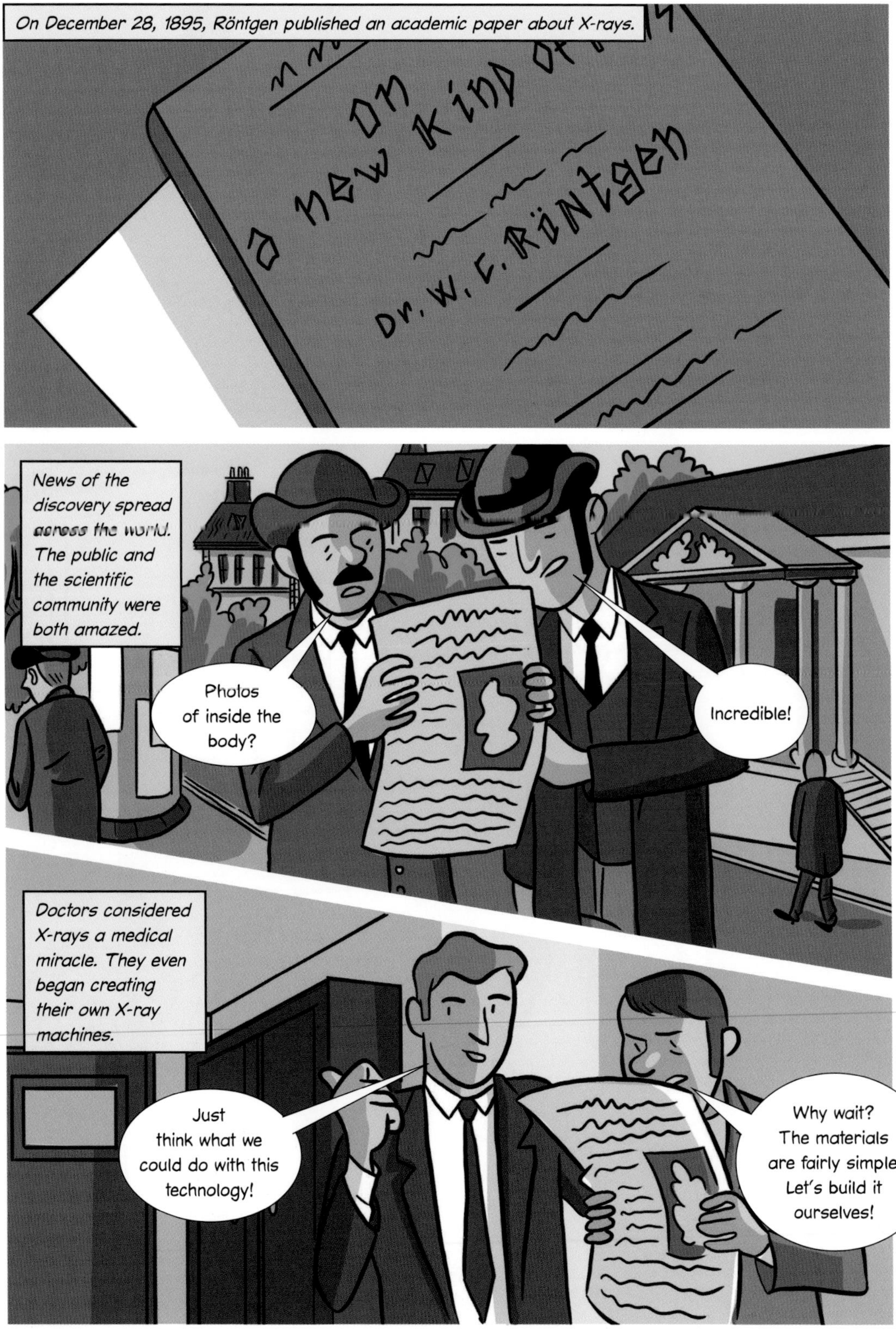
On December 28, 1895, Röntgen published an academic paper about X-rays.
On
a new Kind of
Dr. W. C. Röntgen
News of the discovery spread across the world. The public and the scientific community were both amazed.
Photos of inside the body?
Incredible!
Doctors considered X-rays a medical miracle. They even began creating their own X-ray machines.
Just think what we could do with this technology!
Why wait? The materials are fairly simple. Let's build it ourselves!

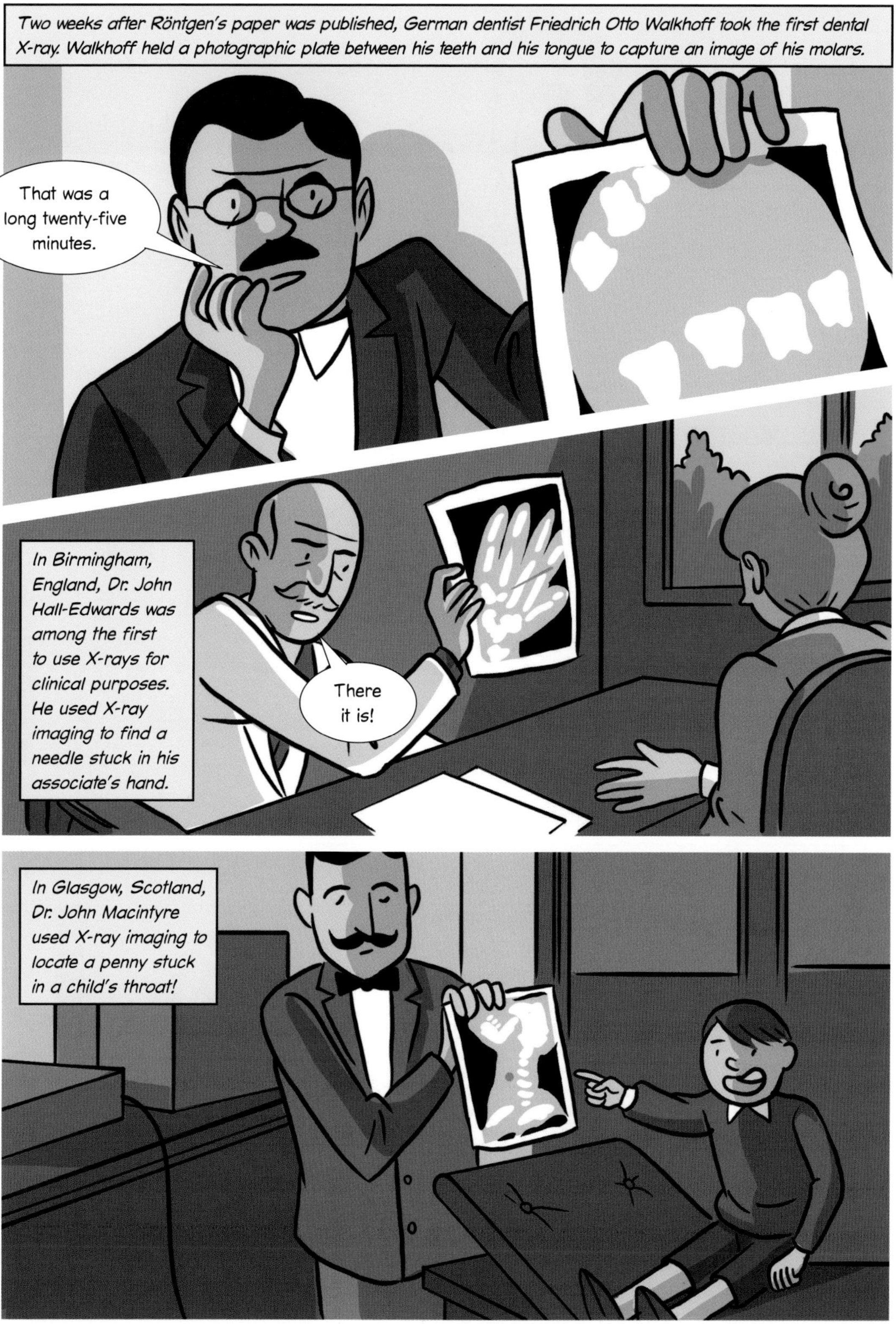
Two weeks after Röntgen's paper was published, German dentist Friedrich Otto Walkhoff took the first dental X-ray. Walkhoff held a photographic plate between his teeth and his tongue to capture an image of his molars.
That was a long twenty-five minutes.
In Birmingham, England, Dr. John Hall-Edwards was among the first to use X-rays for clinical purposes. He used X-ray imaging to find a needle stuck in his associate's hand.
There it is!
In Glasgow, Scotland, Dr. John Macintyre used X-ray imaging to locate a penny stuck in a child's throat!

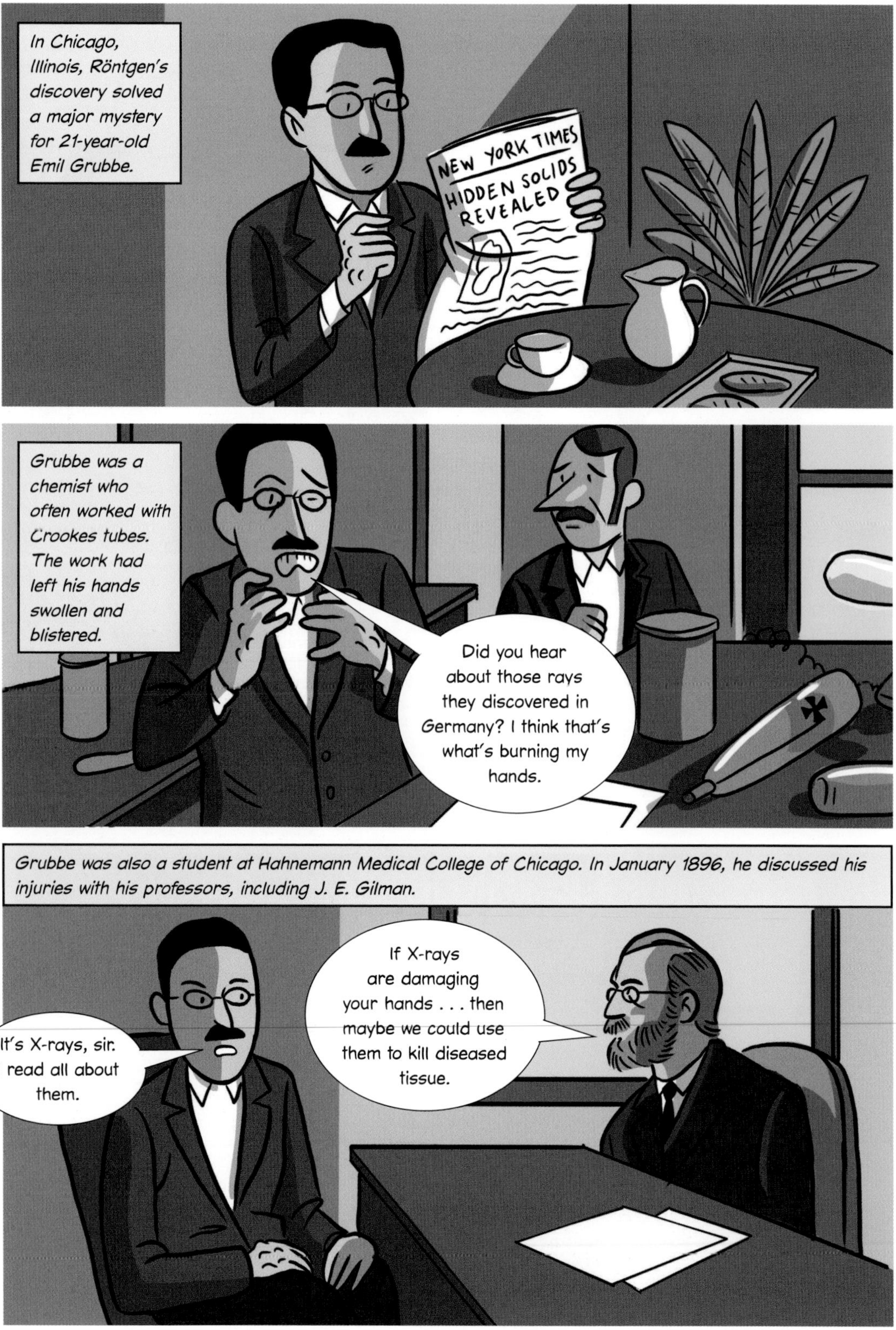
In Chicago, Illinois, Röntgen's discovery solved a major mystery for 21-year-old Emil Grubbe.
NEW YORK TIMES
HIDDEN SOLIDS REVEALED
Grubbe was a chemist who often worked with Crookes tubes. The work had left his hands swollen and blistered.
Did you hear about those rays they discovered in Germany? I think that's what's burning my hands.
Grubbe was also a student at Hahnemann Medical College of Chicago. In January 1896, he discussed his injuries with his professors, including J. E. Gilman.
It's X-rays, sir. I read all about them.
If X-rays are damaging your hands . . . then maybe we could use them to kill diseased tissue.

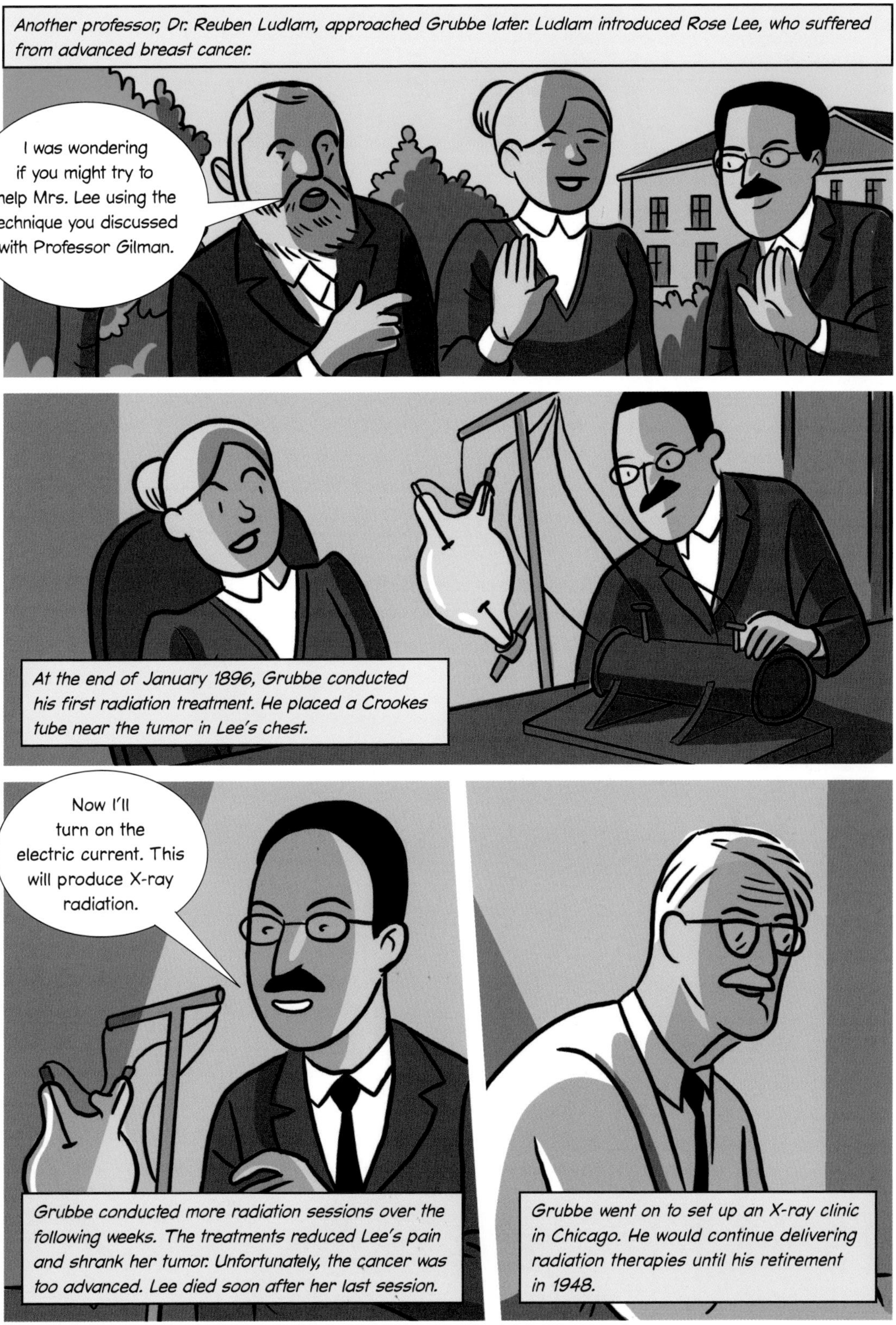
Another professor, Dr. Reuben Ludlam, approached Grubbe later. Ludlam introduced Rose Lee, who suffered from advanced breast cancer.
I was wondering if you might try to help Mrs. Lee using the technique you discussed with Professor Gilman.
At the end of January 1896, Grubbe conducted his first radiation treatment. He placed a Crookes tube near the tumor in Lee's chest.
Now I'll turn on the electric current. This will produce X-ray radiation.
Grubbe conducted more radiation sessions over the following weeks. The treatments reduced Lee's pain and shrank her tumor. Unfortunately, the cancer was too advanced. Lee died soon after her last session.
Grubbe went on to set up an X-ray clinic in Chicago. He would continue delivering radiation therapies until his retirement in 1948.

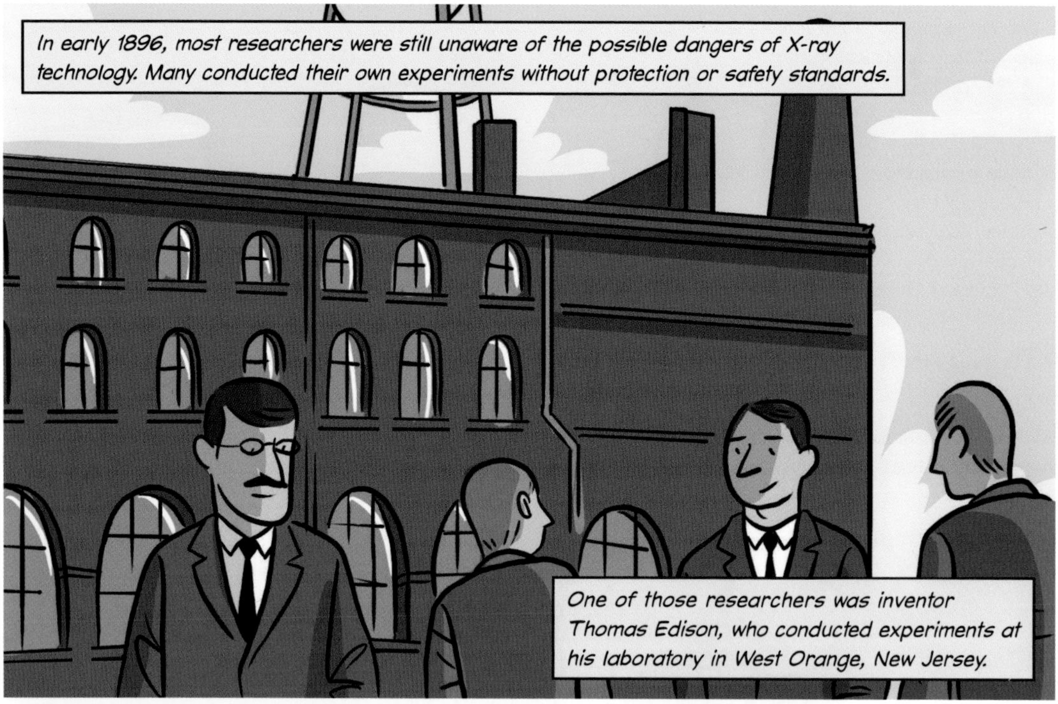
In early 1896, most researchers were still unaware of the possible dangers of X-ray technology. Many conducted their own experiments without protection or safety standards.
One of those researchers was inventor Thomas Edison, who conducted experiments at his laboratory in West Orange, New Jersey.

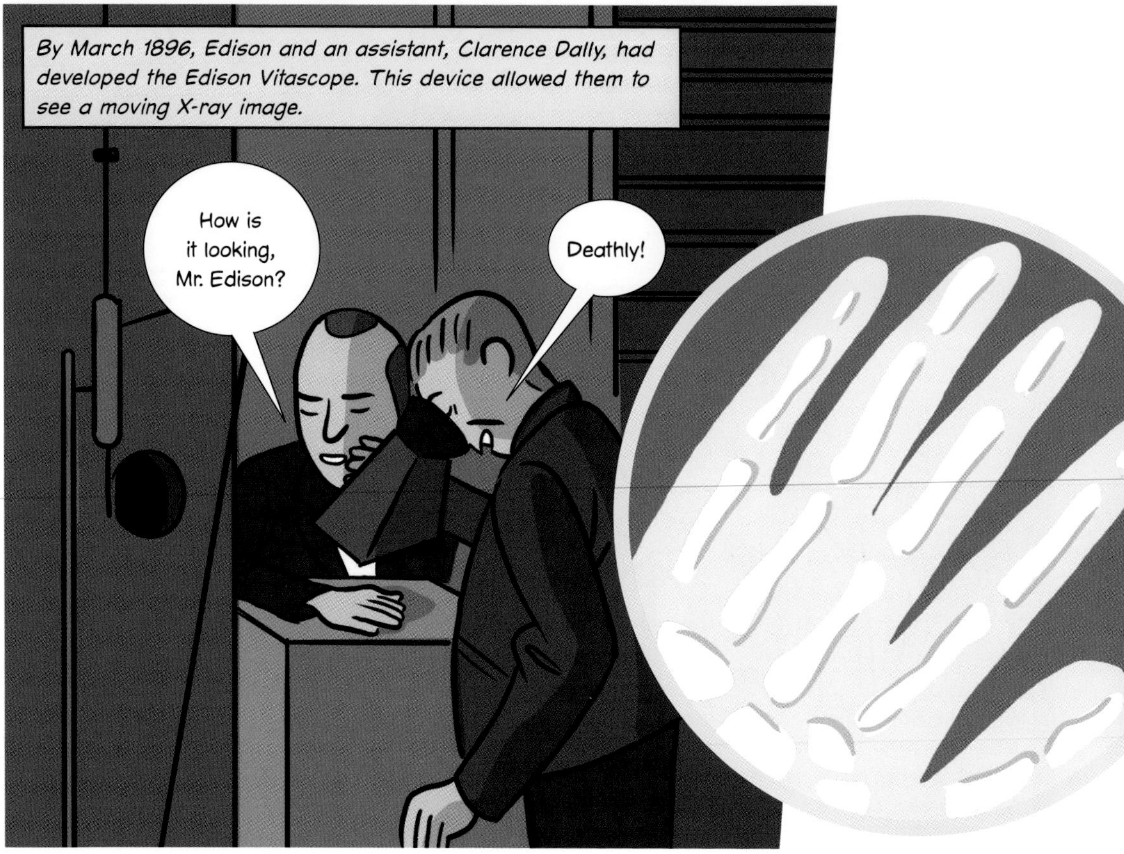
By March 1896, Edison and an assistant, Clarence Dally, had developed the Edison Vitascope. This device allowed them to see a moving X-ray image.
How is it looking, Mr. Edison?
Deathly!

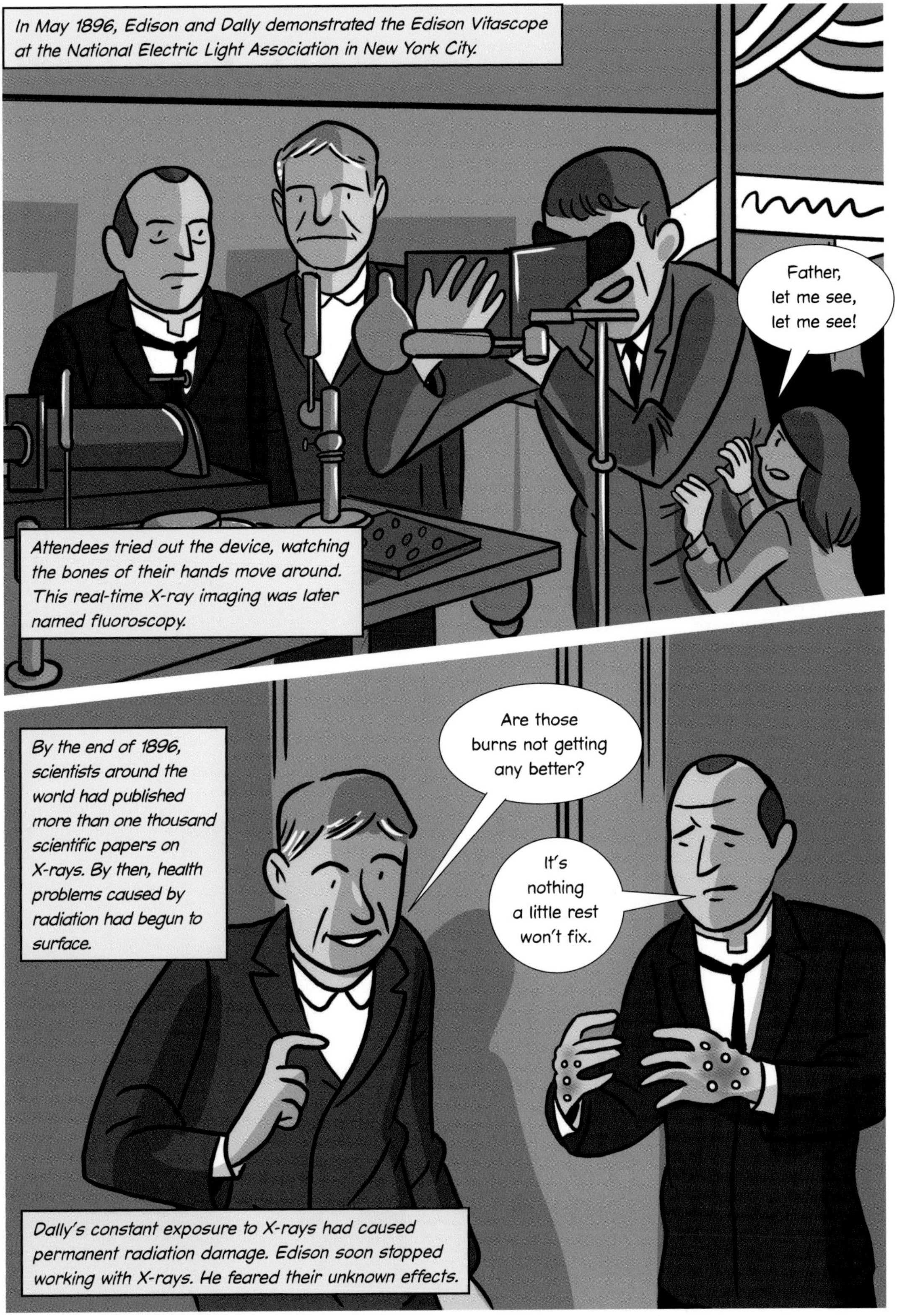
In May 1896, Edison and Dally demonstrated the Edison Vitascope at the National Electric Light Association in New York City.
Father, let me see, let me see!
Attendees tried out the device, watching the bones of their hands move around. This real-time X-ray imaging was later named fluoroscopy.
By the end of 1896, scientists around the world had published more than one thousand scientific papers on X-rays. By then, health problems caused by radiation had begun to surface.
Are those burns not getting any better?
It's nothing a little rest won't fix.
Dally's constant exposure to X-rays had caused permanent radiation damage. Edison soon stopped working with X-rays. He feared their unknown effects.

CHAPTER 3: INVISIBLE DANGERS

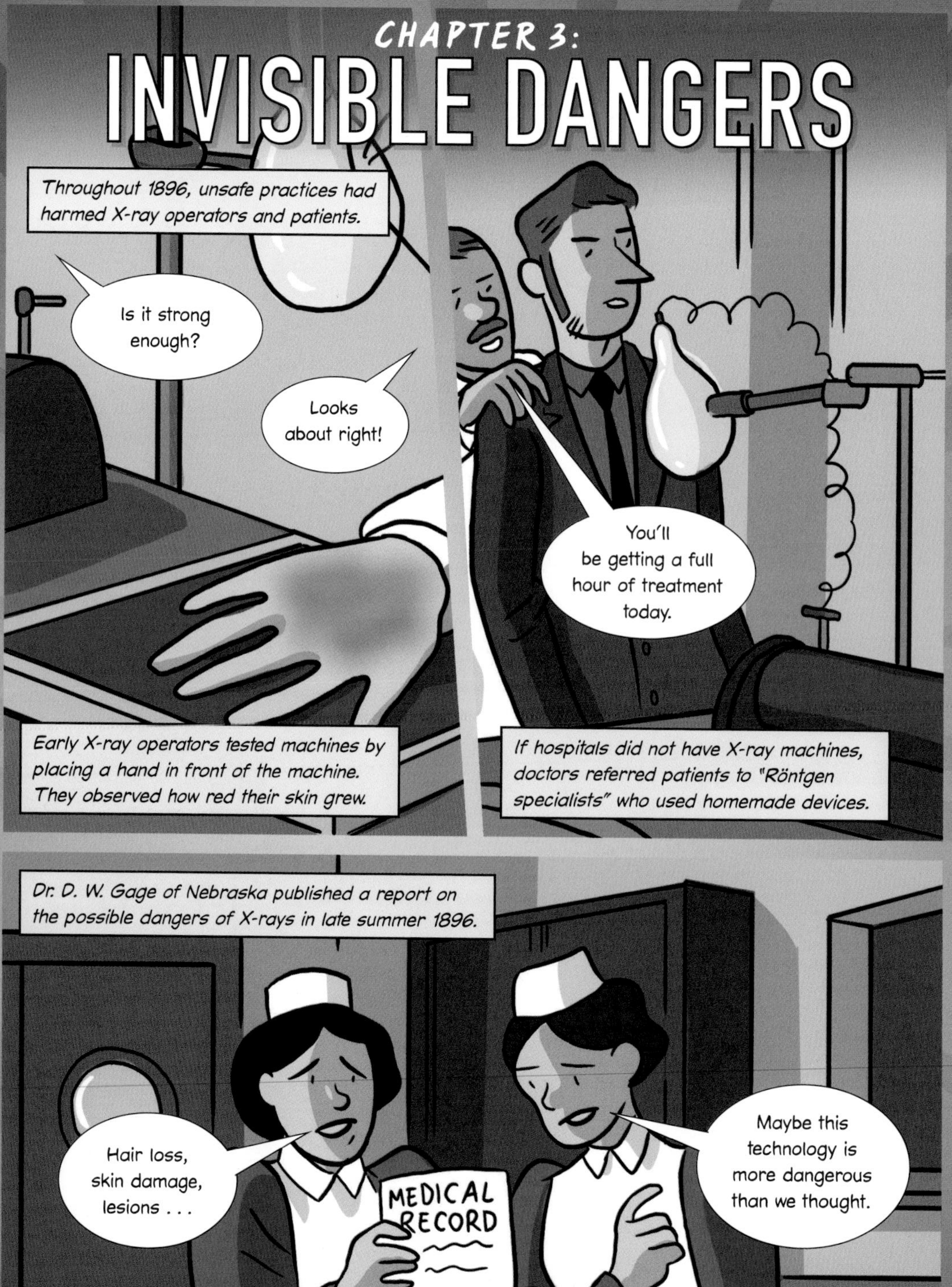

Throughout 1896, unsafe practices had harmed X-ray operators and patients.
Is it strong enough?
Looks about right!
Early X-ray operators tested machines by placing a hand in front of the machine. They observed how red their skin grew.
You'll be getting a full hour of treatment today.
If hospitals did not have X-ray machines, doctors referred patients to "Röntgen specialists" who used homemade devices.
Dr. D. W. Gage of Nebraska published a report on the possible dangers of X-rays in late summer 1896.
Hair loss, skin damage, lesions . . .
MEDICAL RECORD
Maybe this technology is more dangerous than we thought.

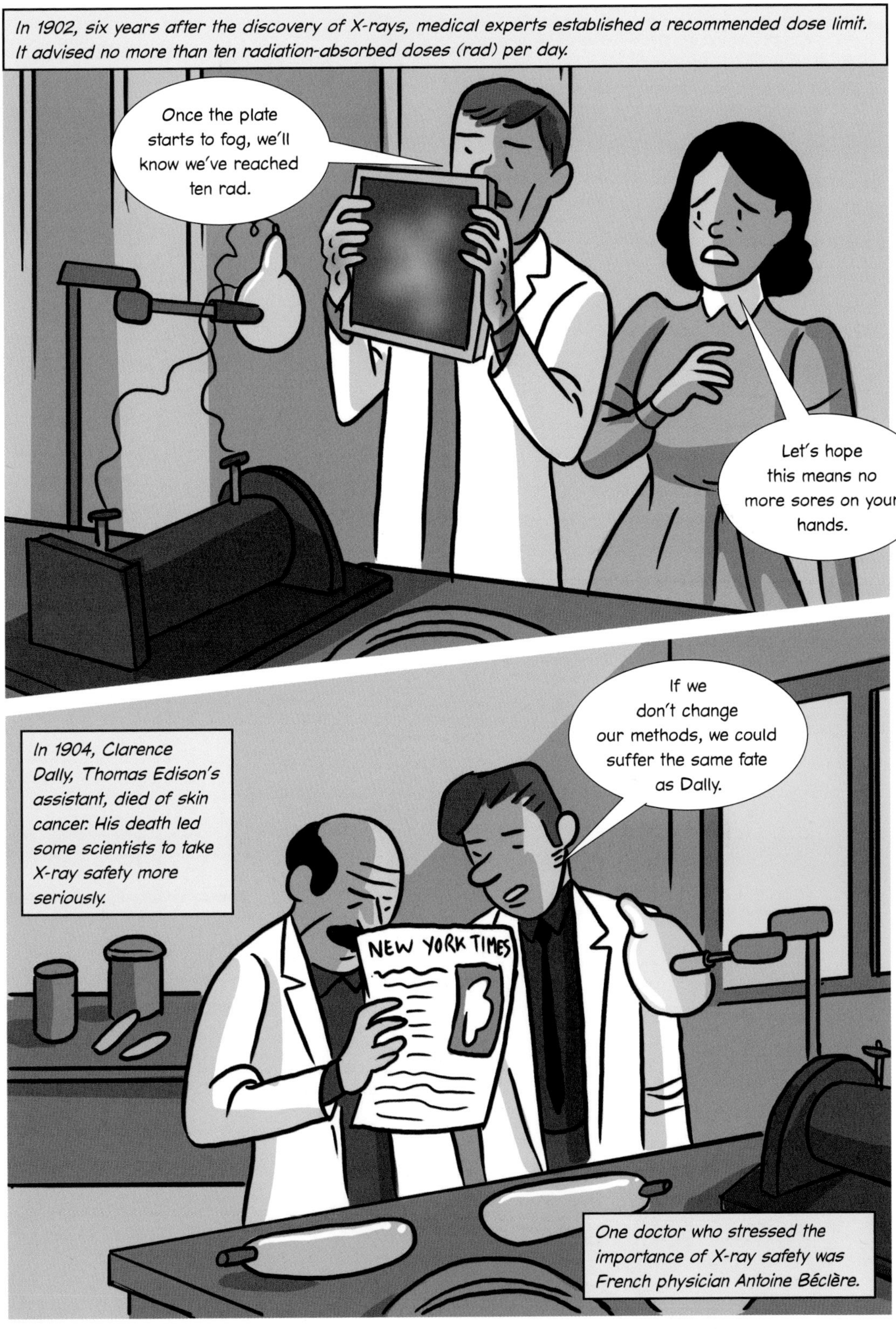
In 1902, six years after the discovery of X-rays, medical experts established a recommended dose limit. It advised no more than ten radiation-absorbed doses (rad) per day.
Once the plate starts to fog, we'll know we've reached ten rad.
Let's hope this means no more sores on your hands.
In 1904, Clarence Dally, Thomas Edison's assistant, died of skin cancer. His death led some scientists to take X-ray safety more seriously.
If we don't change our methods, we could suffer the same fate as Dally.
NEW YORK TIMES
One doctor who stressed the importance of X-ray safety was French physician Antoine Béclère.

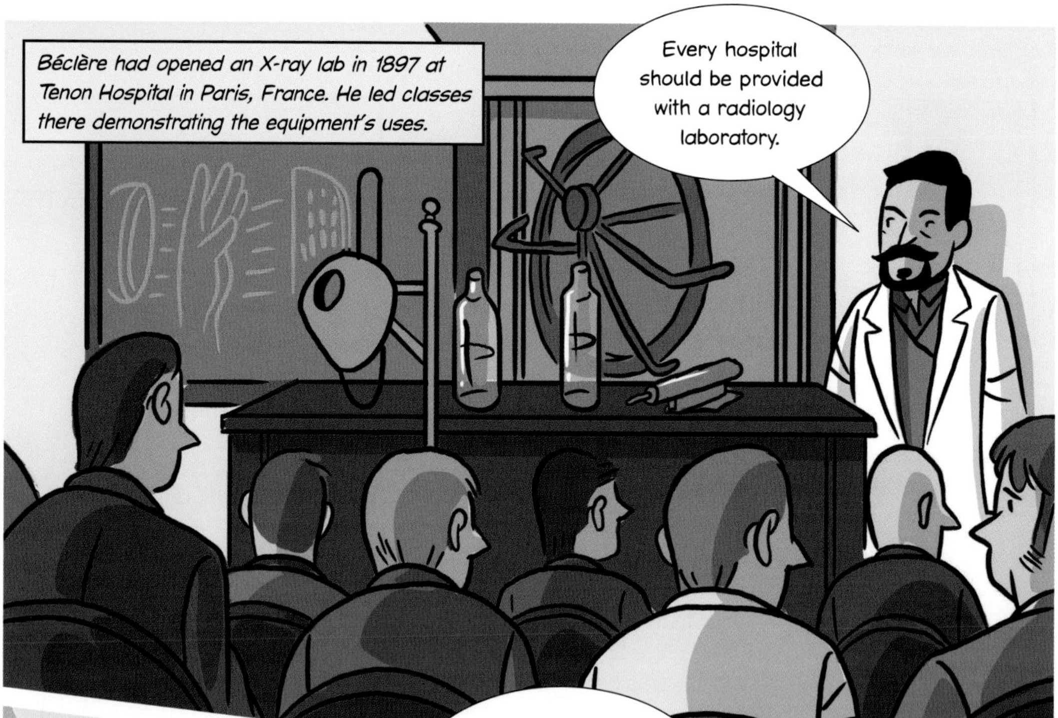
Béclère had opened an X-ray lab in 1897 at Tenon Hospital in Paris, France. He led classes there demonstrating the equipment's uses.
Every hospital should be provided with a radiology laboratory.

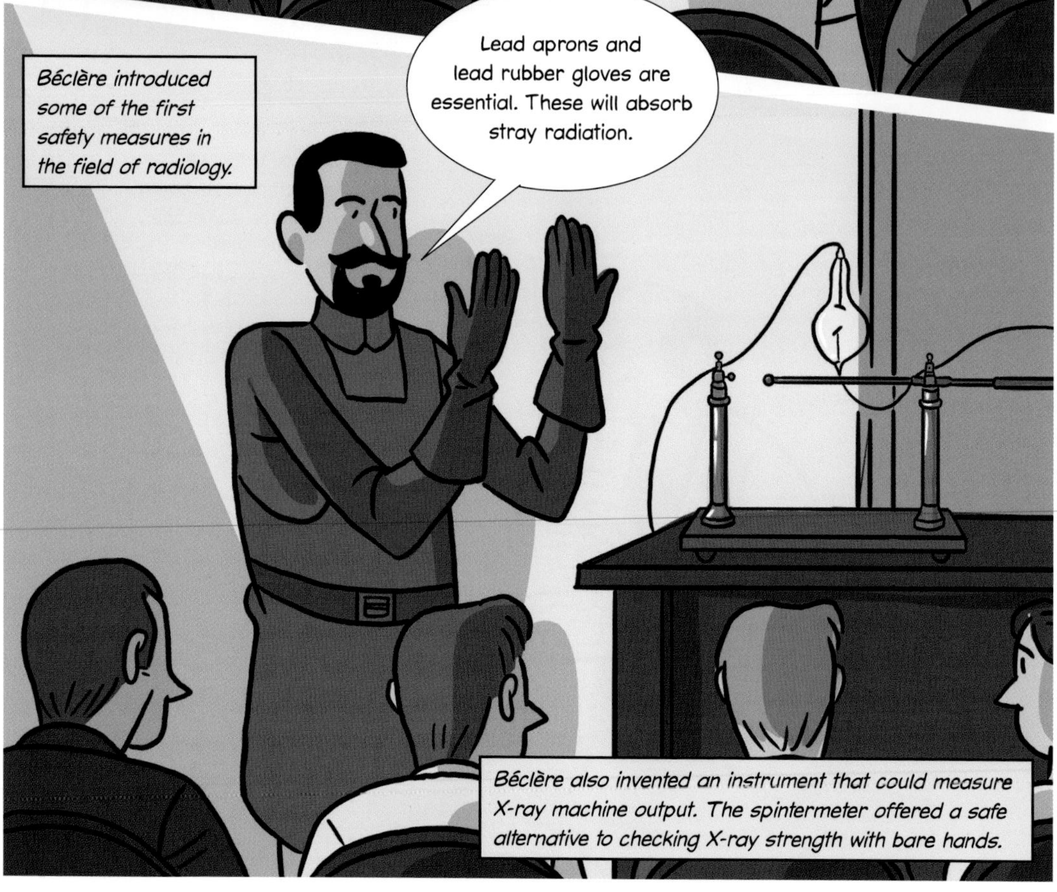
Béclère introduced some of the first safety measures in the field of radiology.
Lead aprons and lead rubber gloves are essential. These will absorb stray radiation.
Béclère also invented an instrument that could measure X-ray machine output. The spintermeter offered a safe alternative to checking X-ray strength with bare hands.

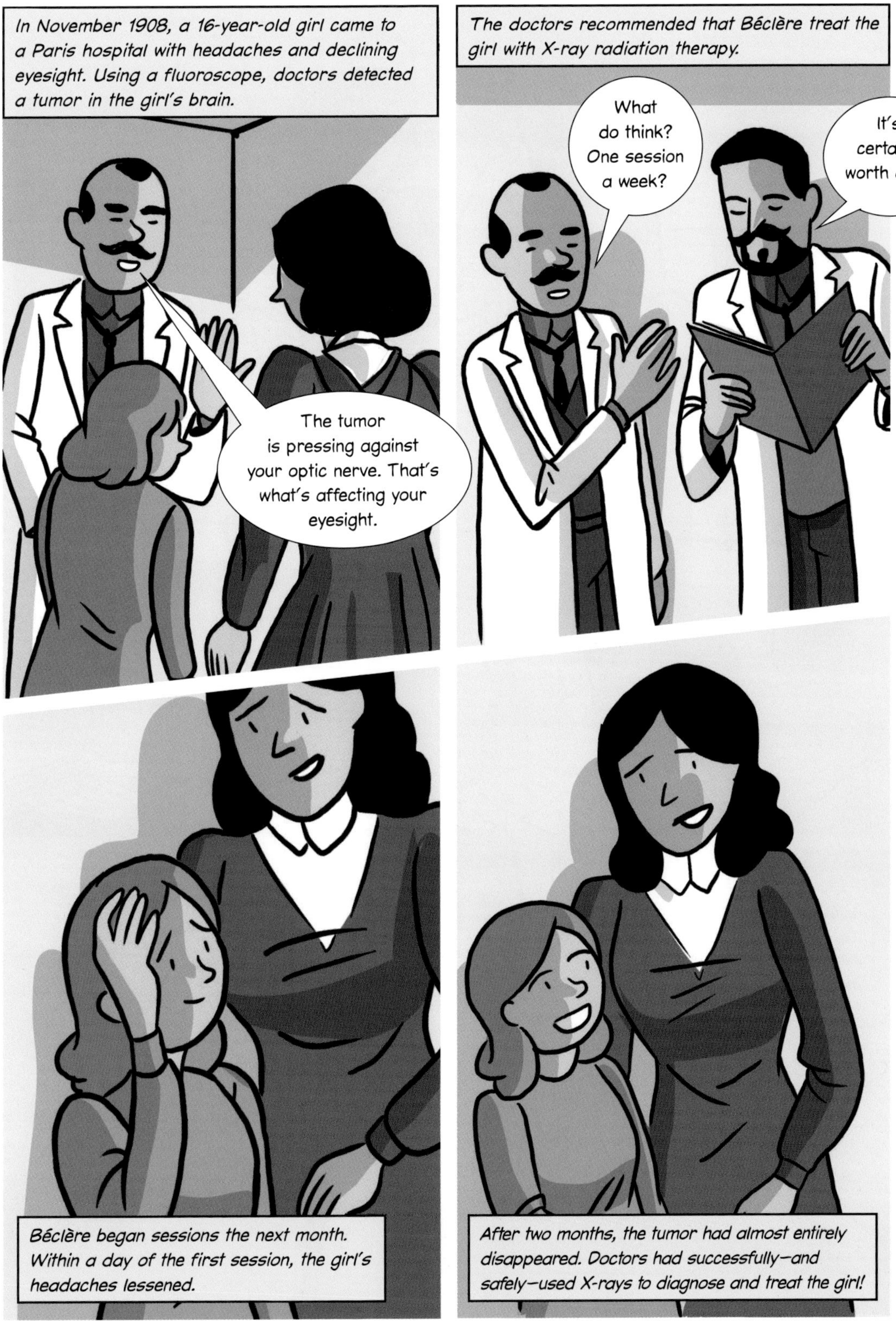
In November 1908, a 16-year-old girl came to a Paris hospital with headaches and declining eyesight. Using a fluoroscope, doctors detected a tumor in the girl's brain.
The tumor is pressing against your optic nerve. That's what's affecting your eyesight.
The doctors recommended that Béclère treat the girl with X-ray radiation therapy.
What do think? One session a week?
It's certainly worth a try.
Béclère began sessions the next month. Within a day of the first session, the girl's headaches lessened.
After two months, the tumor had almost entirely disappeared. Doctors had successfully—and safely—used X-rays to diagnose and treat the girl!

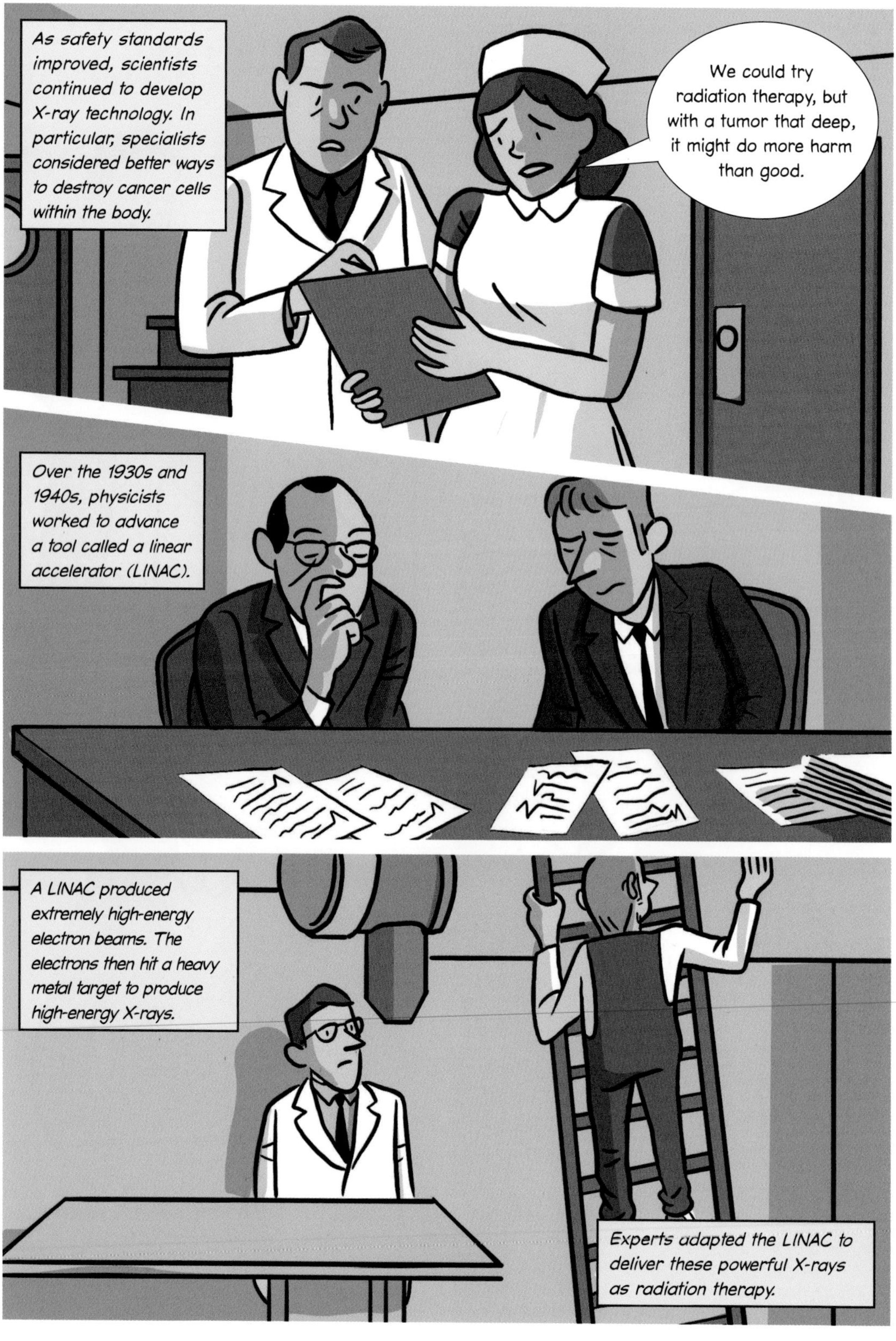
As safety standards improved, scientists continued to develop X-ray technology. In particular, specialists considered better ways to destroy cancer cells within the body.
We could try radiation therapy, but with a tumor that deep, it might do more harm than good.
Over the 1930s and 1940s, physicists worked to advance a tool called a linear accelerator (LINAC).
A LINAC produced extremely high-energy electron beams. The electrons then hit a heavy metal target to produce high-energy X-rays.
Experts adapted the LINAC to deliver these powerful X-rays as radiation therapy.

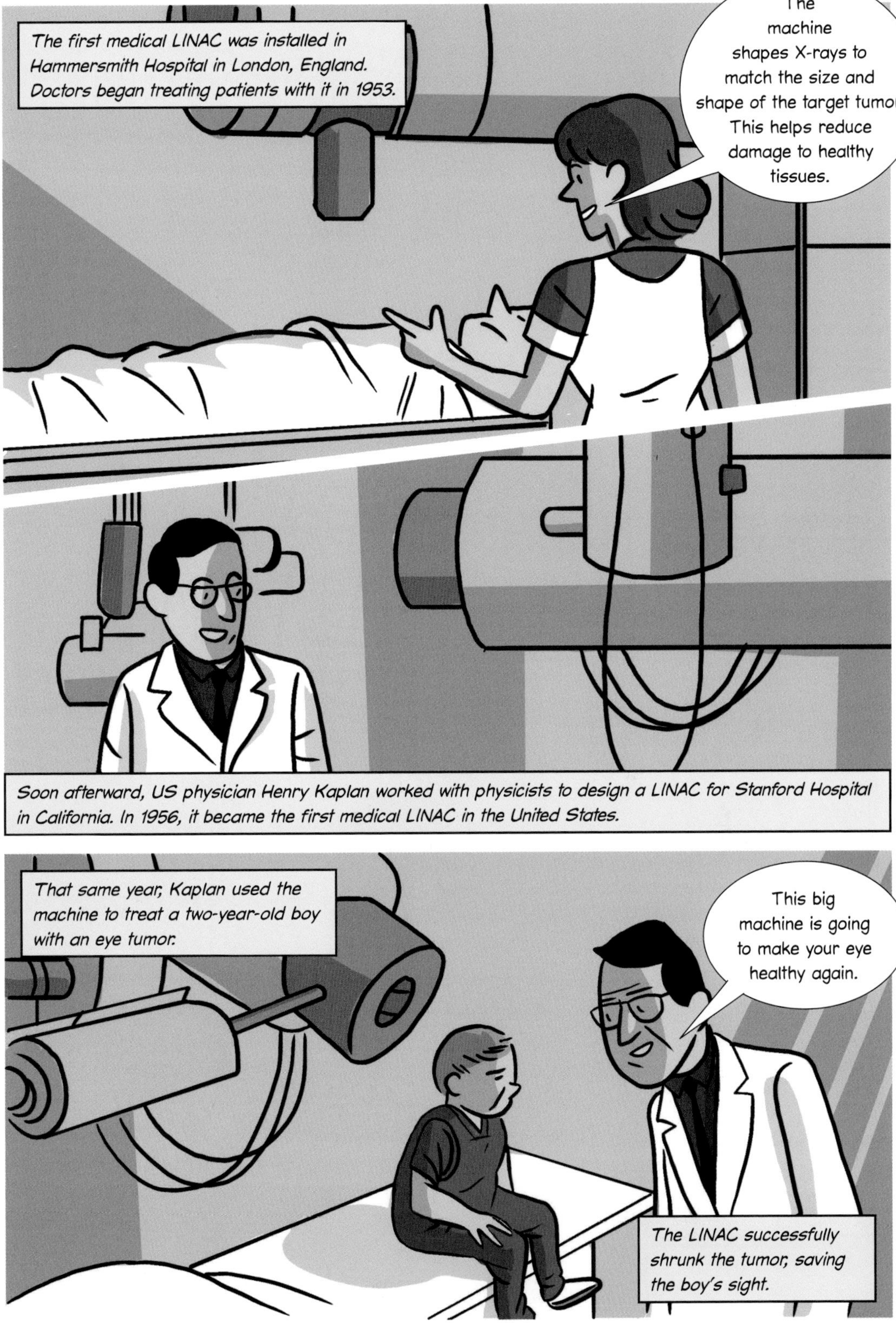
The first medical LINAC was installed in Hammersmith Hospital in London, England. Doctors began treating patients with it in 1953.
The machine shapes X-rays to match the size and shape of the target tumor. This helps reduce damage to healthy tissues.
Soon afterward, US physician Henry Kaplan worked with physicists to design a LINAC for Stanford Hospital in California. In 1956, it became the first medical LINAC in the United States.
That same year, Kaplan used the machine to treat a two-year-old boy with an eye tumor.
This big machine is going to make your eye healthy again.
The LINAC successfully shrunk the tumor, saving the boy's sight.

CHAPTER 4:
CT SCANS AND COLOR

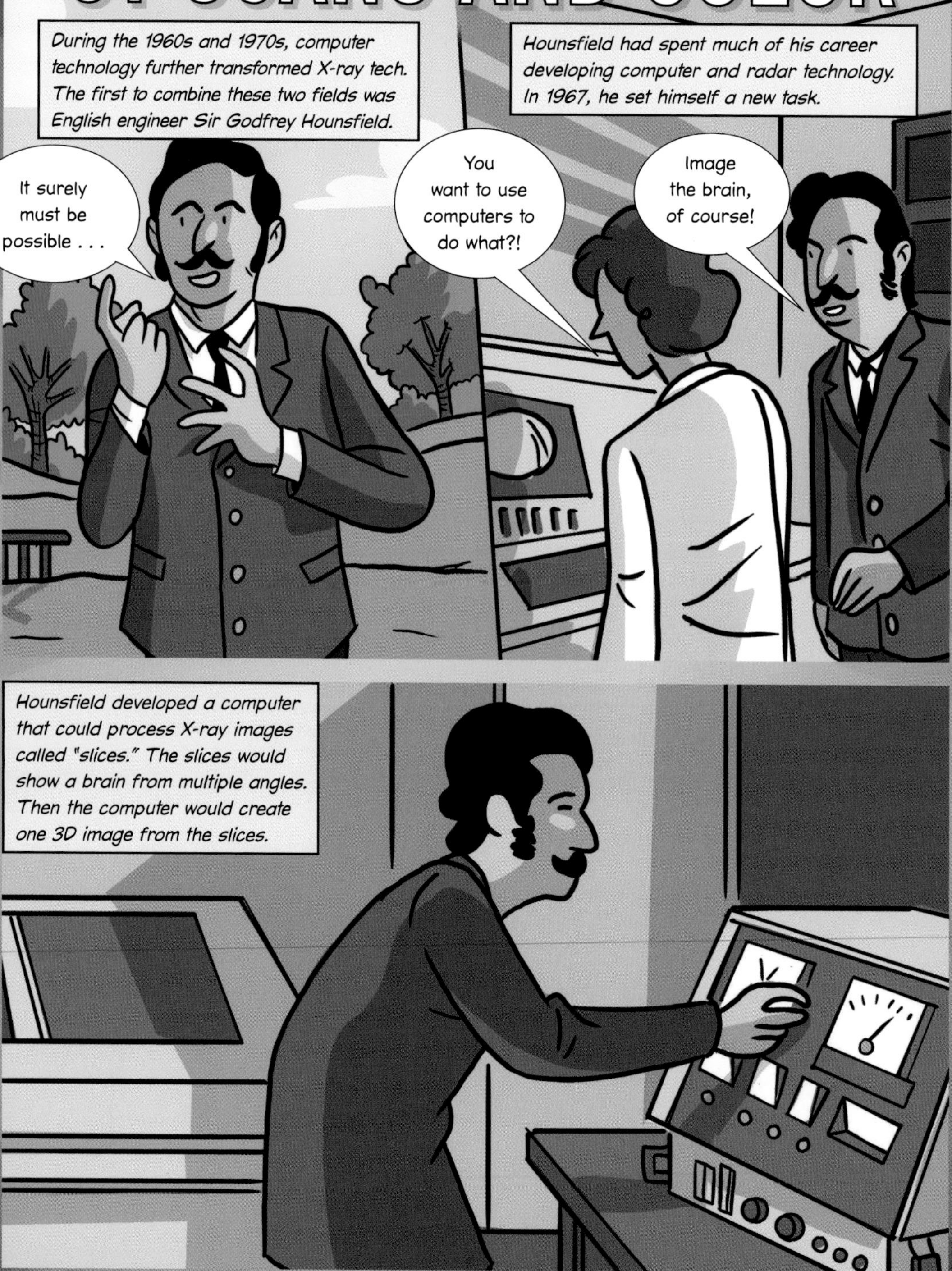
During the 1960s and 1970s, computer technology further transformed X-ray tech. The first to combine these two fields was English engineer Sir Godfrey Hounsfield.
It surely must be possible . . .
Hounsfield had spent much of his career developing computer and radar technology. In 1967, he set himself a new task.
You want to use computers to do what?!
Image the brain, of course!
Hounsfield developed a computer that could process X-ray images called "slices." The slices would show a brain from multiple angles. Then the computer would create one 3D image from the slices.

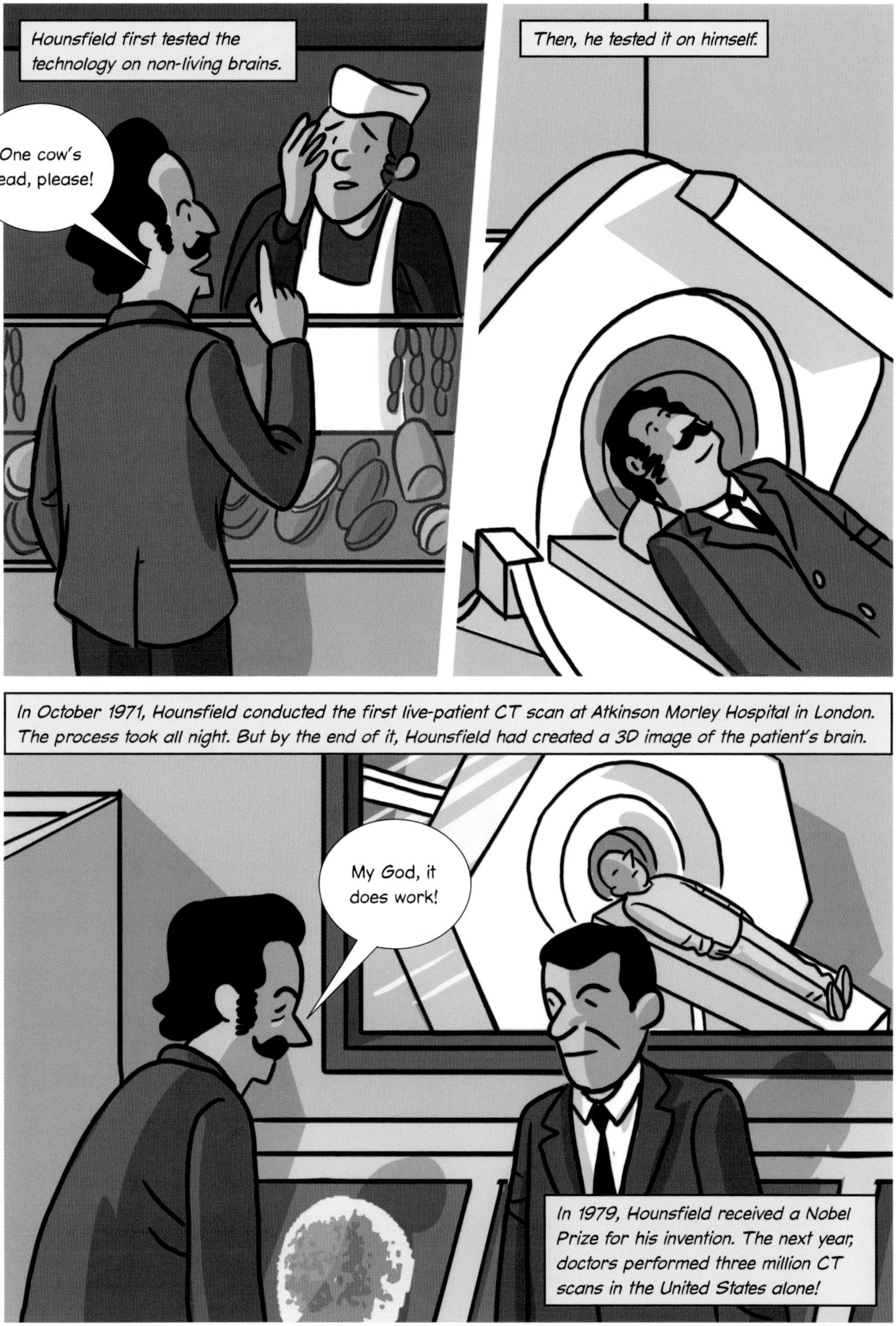
Hounsfield first tested the technology on non-living brains.
One cow's head, please!
Then, he tested it on himself.
In October 1971, Hounsfield conducted the first live-patient CT scan at Atkinson Morley Hospital in London. The process took all night. But by the end of it, Hounsfield had created a 3D image of the patient's brain.
My God, it does work!
In 1979, Hounsfield received a Nobel Prize for his invention. The next year, doctors performed three million CT scans in the United States alone!

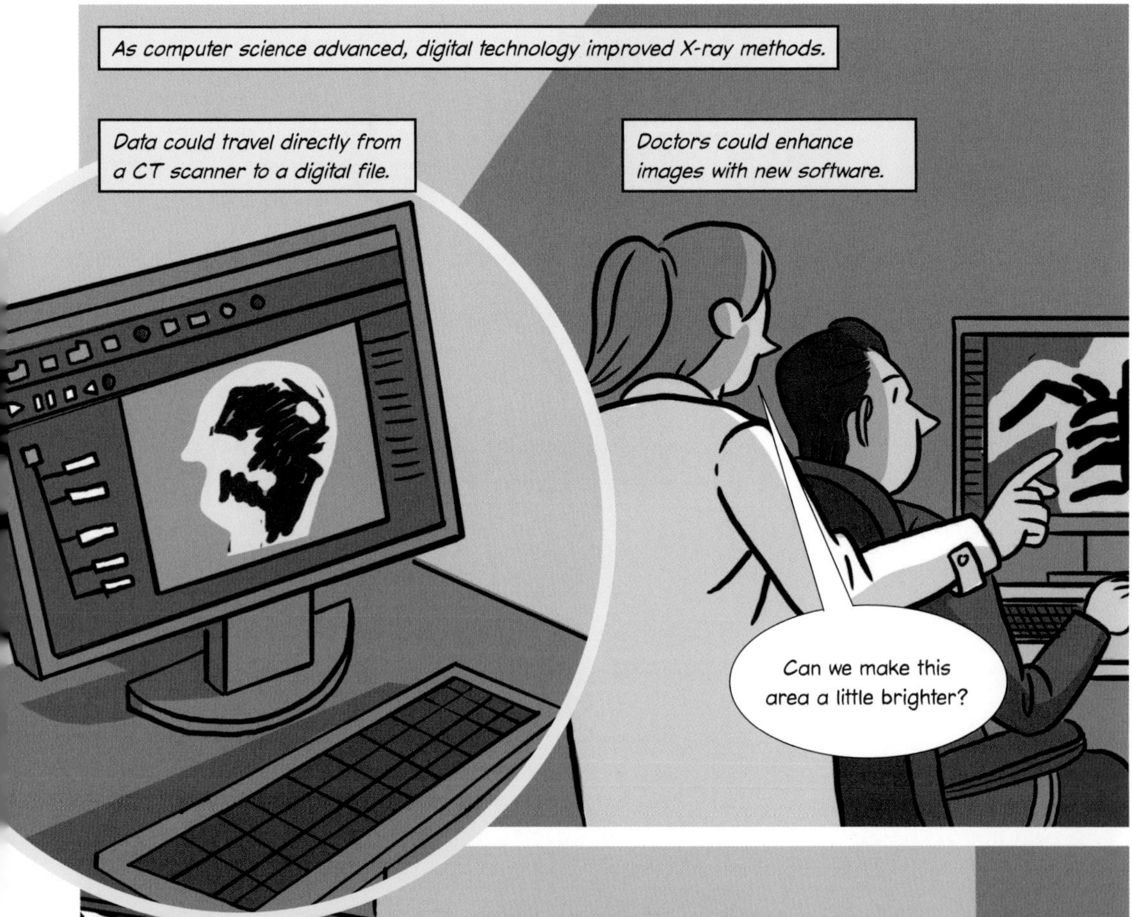
As computer science advanced, digital technology improved X-ray methods.
Data could travel directly from a CT scanner to a digital file.
Doctors could enhance images with new software.
Can we make this area a little brighter?

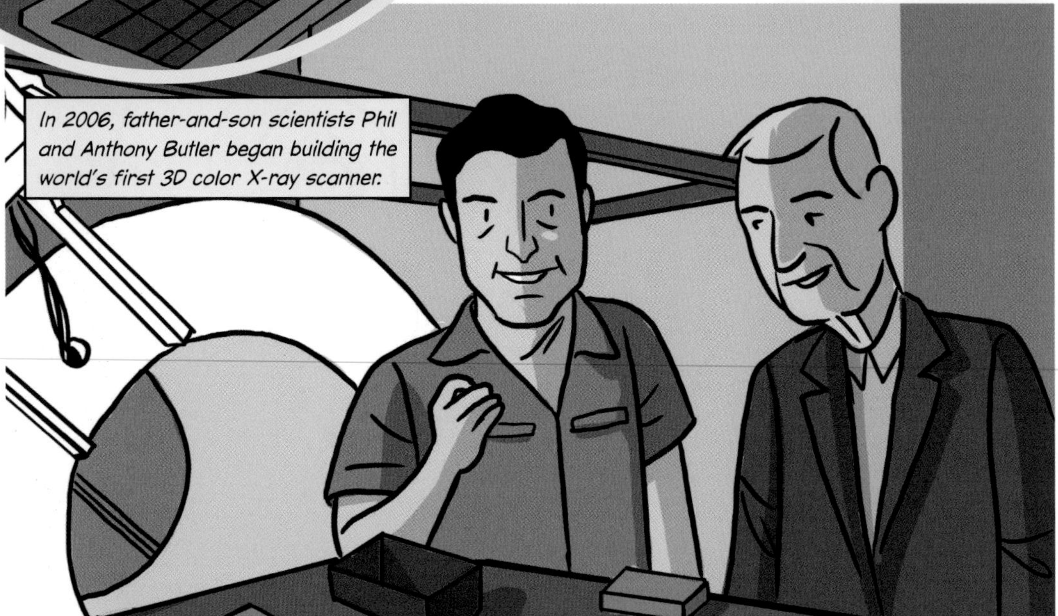
In 2006, father-and-son scientists Phil and Anthony Butler began building the world's first 3D color X-ray scanner.

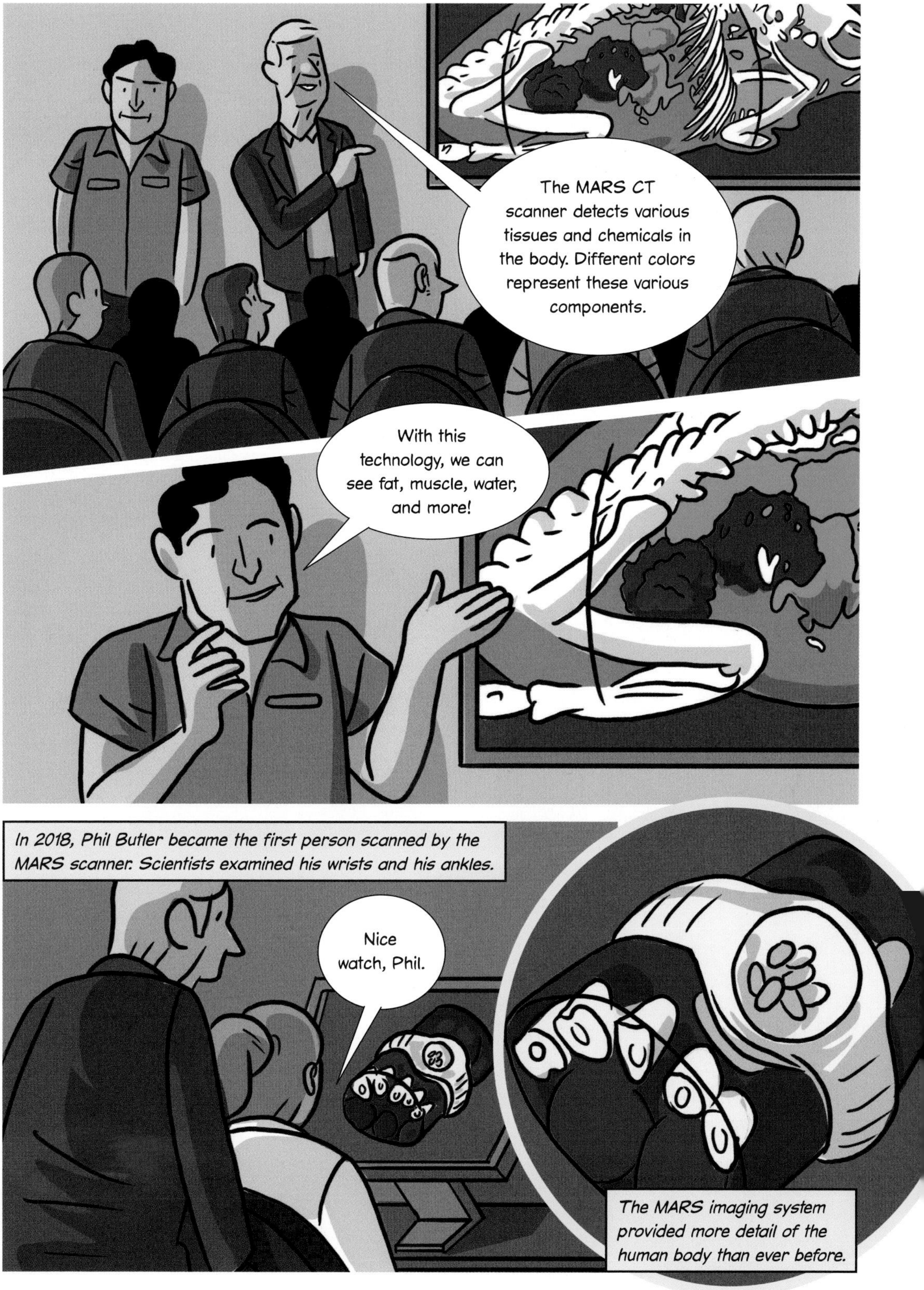
The MARS CT scanner detects various tissues and chemicals in the body. Different colors represent these various components.
With this technology, we can see fat, muscle, water, and more!
In 2018, Phil Butler became the first person scanned by the MARS scanner. Scientists examined his wrists and his ankles.
Nice watch, Phil.
The MARS imaging system provided more detail of the human body than ever before.

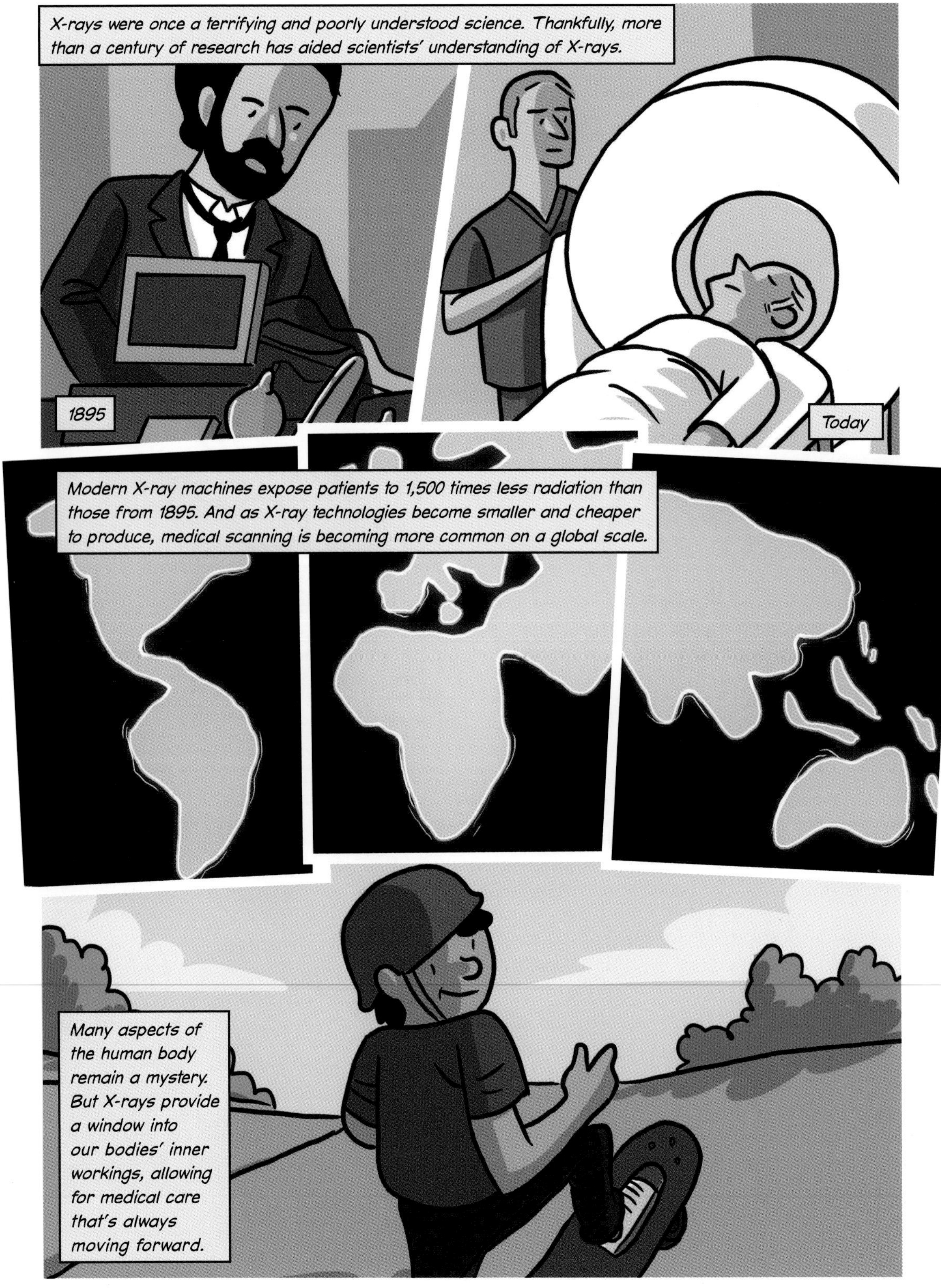

X-rays were once a terrifying and poorly understood science. Thankfully, more than a century of research has aided scientists' understanding of X-rays.
1895
Today
Modern X-ray machines expose patients to 1,500 times less radiation than those from 1895. And as X-ray technologies become smaller and cheaper to produce, medical scanning is becoming more common on a global scale.
Many aspects of the human body remain a mystery. But X-rays provide a window into our bodies' inner workings, allowing for medical care that's always moving forward.

SOURCE NOTES

8   Dr. Howard Markel, "The Dirty, Painful Death of President James A. Garfield," *PBS News Hour*, September 16, 2016, https://www.pbs.org/newshour/health/dirty-painful-death -president-james-garfield.

11 Dr. Howard Markel, "'I Have Seen My Death': How the World Discovered the X-Ray," *PBS News Hour*, December 20, 2012, https://www.pbs.org/newshour/health/i-have-seen -my-death-how-the-world-discovered-the-x-ray.

25 Lawrence R. Goodman, "The Beatles, the Nobel Prize, and CT Scanning of the Chest," *Radiologic Clinics of North America*, January 2010, Volume 48, Issue 1, page 1, https://www.sciencedirect.com/sdfe/pdf/download /eid/1-s2.0-S0033838909000178X/first-page-pdf.

GLOSSARY

cancer: an often-deadly disease in which abnormal cells grow in the body and destroy healthy organs

clinical: relating to the treatment of patients

diagnose: to recognize a disease or illness in someone

electron: a small particle that has a negative electric charge and travels around the nucleus of an atom. When electrons flow between atoms, they produce an electric current.

lesion: any damage or abnormal change to healthy tissues, such as the tissues that make up the skin

Nobel Prize: an annual award given to people who have done important work in their fields

optic nerve: a band of sensory tissue in the back of the eye that sends visual information from the eye to the brain

physicist: a person who studies physics, the science of matter and energy

radar: a device that uses radio waves to detect distant objects, such as airplanes or ships

radiation: energy given off from a source in the form of invisible waves or rays

radiology: a branch of medicine that uses radiation, such as X-rays, to diagnose and treat illnesses and injuries

retirement: the act of retiring, or ending one's professional career

software: computer programs that perform specific functions

tumor: an abnormal lump or mass of cells in the body

vacuum: an empty space containing no air or other gases

FURTHER INFORMATION

Alma Kids—The Electromagnetic Spectrum
https://kids.alma.cl/the-electromagnetic-spectrum/

Britannica Kids—X-rays
https://kids.britannica.com/kids/article/X-rays/353941

Choudhury, Bipasha. *Human Body*. New York: DK Publishing, 2017.

Horstschäfer, Felicitas. *X-ray Me! Look Inside Your Body*. New York: Greenwillow Books, 2019.

TED-Ed—How X-rays See Through Your Skin
https://www.youtube.com/watch?v=gsV7SJDDCY4

Wojton, Nick. *Oops! They're X-rays!* New York: Gareth Stevens Publishing, 2020.

INDEX